AGENCY PROCEDURES;
LUST and CORRUPTION

BY

M. J. DAVIS

ISBN: 1-4033-0380-0 (e-book)
ISBN: 1-4033-0381-9 (Paperback)
ISBN: 1-4033-4099-4 (Hardcover)

Library of Congress control Number: 2002101927

This book is printed on acid free paper.

Printed in the United States of America
Bloomington, IN

Cover art by M. J.Davis
Cover design by Mamie Davis

1stBooks - rev. 06/20/02

"Pentecost shows that humans can learn to think as God does. It reminds us that we as God's chosen people are the first to take part in God's specific purpose on earth."

But
some of us are <u>not</u> aware of this divine truth! Therefore I am bringing forth the following story, based upon factual situations.

Dedicated to my family,
JJB, CJS, CJB, and JCR who helped me
to get this book together.

TABLE OF CONTENTS

1991

The Demise of Agatha Fluddrucker

It was 8 A.M. The two cleaning men, Tony and Jerry, had just arrived on the fourth floor. They had finished cleaning every other office in the building, except Agatha Fluddrucker's, saving her office for last. She and her friends did peculiar things there in the mornings before the rest of the staff reported for work at the Bureau of Communications and Systems. (BCS)

Four years earlier, Agatha started a love-hate relationship with her assistant Emmaline Spenser.

BCS staff started hot rumors about the two of them. Not until Tony and Jerry caught Agatha and Emmaline in a compromising position were the rumors verified, at least by the cleaning men. Agatha had screamed obscenities at them and vowed to have them fired if they told anybody.

It was the second time that Agatha was caught in a compromising situation. The other time was in a different *agency* with a *man* half her age.

Now, at BCS, she was up to her old tricks again. When Tony and Jerry walked in on Emmaline and Agatha, it was 7 A.M. Who knew the women were there? At that time of the morning the place was usually empty except for the cleaning personnel. If they wanted total privacy, they should have gone to a motel.

As Tony and Jerry approached Agatha's office *this* morning, they were almost frozen with fear and anxiety. The lights were on in there; they could hear the radio playing.

They stood still outside the door, like statues, not moving. She should have been finished playing her games by now. They had given her plenty of time, the office had to be cleaned. The supervising custodian would show up soon to inspect the offices.

Tony, the braver of the two (for the moment), timidly knocked on the door to Agatha's office.

No answer.

He knocked again, this time a little louder.

Still no answer.

"Mrs. Fluddrucker?"

The silence was ominous. She should have been cursing them out by now.

"Mrs. Fluddrucker, are you in there? If you don't answer now, we're coming in. We have to finish up cleaning, that's our job."

There was no answer to this last query. Still hesitant they decided to take a chance and go in anyway.

Tony led, since he was the larger of the two men. It was taken for granted that that fact made him the bravest. This suited Jerry just fine. He needed his job to support his wife and kids.

Walking into the office with great caution, Tony nervously glanced around the room. Not seeing Agatha, he breathed a deep sigh of relief. Going around the back of the desk, he stopped in his tracks, eyes locking on Agatha's lifeless body.

Agatha's orange-red hair was standing on end, looking worse in death than it did in life. Her eyes, looked worse. They bulged even more. Agatha's lips were frozen in a screaming position. His view of her bloody face was beginning to build up an overwhelming terror and nausea in Tony.

It was the eyes that really shattered Tony. They seemed to come right out of the sockets at him. He stared back at them, paralyzed to the spot. Heavy sweat began to pour from his armpits and down his face, which had turned pale from shock.

He began to retreat slowly from what remained of Agatha. The initial shock of seeing her like that was being replaced by pure fear. He realized the killer could still be in the building.

Jerry hanging back outside the office, was unaware of Tony's grisly discovery, and called out "Mrs. Fluddrucker?"

"She aint ever gonna' answer you, Jerry." Tony's voice was shaking badly.

"How the hell do *you* know? Maybe she's in the toilet."

"She ain't in the toilet. We have to call the police, come over here."

Jerry walked over and looked down at the body. The grotesque form of Agatha Fluddrucker made his hair stand up on end.

"JEEZ!" Jerry's eyes were bulging almost as badly as Agatha's.

Meanwhile, downstairs, an unseen individual slipped out of the building.

1973

The Chronicles of Sheba Welters at County Bureau # 105

It was a sweltering hot day in the city. The local welfare center, County Bureau #105, had no air conditioning, just one or two large fans on each of its five floors. The place was jammed with impatient, overheated clients and their children, getting ready to explode at high noon.

Sheba Welters, one of the two group supervisors on the first floor, surveyed the situation as small beads of perspiration rolled down her forehead.

In 1973 the city was installing its first automated welfare system to make processing clients' checks faster and more cost effective. Instead, the complex conversion from the manual system to the automatic system was becoming fouled up and complicated. Checks were going out late or shortchanged. Some had gone to the wrong address. To complicate the situation further, a few clients were trying to get checks they were not entitled to receive.

In the client's waiting area, an angry mother was threatening to abandon her six children in the center. The four oldest children sat looking very sad and very nervous. They didn't want their mother to leave them, no matter how bad she might be. The two youngest, both under 2 years old, were crying at the top of their lungs. None of the children had been fed that day, including the 2 month old baby.

"I don't want my children sleeping on no pissy mattresses." She was screaming over everyone to be heard.

"They stink the whole house up." She failed to realize that new mattresses would not solve the problem as long as her children continued to wet the bed. The state would not allow the County Bureau to issue her the money.

Nobody, including the children, wanted the mother to walk out on her brood. A neglectful mother was better than no mother at all. The social workers were trying to maintain an outward appearance of calm to mask the fact that they were upset. A child placement meant staying overtime, waiting for the children to be placed in a home or shelter.

It was almost lunch hour. Some of the staff were already upstairs in the lounge having lunch. They didn't care how many clients came into the center, that was a problem for the more dedicated personnel.

Meanwhile, Sheba was trying to maintain the peace in her own unit. Being on the first floor put her right in the midst of the hubbub at the County Bureau #105. Management felt that this was the best location for the Aged, Blind and Disabled unit. In 1973 that term disabled also included narcotic addicts and mental patients.

Sheba eyed the row of workers under her supervision, wishing all of her workers were as conscientious as Betty Scully.

It was only the noon hour and, Lord, she was tired.

Not only did she have to contend with upset clients, greedy landlords charging exorbitant rents for substandard housing loaded with rats and cockroaches, moving men who charged as much to move a client's one room as they did an entire house full of furniture, client's children who could well afford to support their elderly parents but preferred to leave them on their own, various outside agencies fighting for clients civil rights, bogus complaints and officious orders issued from the Mayor's office that added to the workload of the center's already overburdened staff, today, of all days, all of the pressures and Sheba's worst behaving employees, Evelyn and Pearl, chose to prove just how uncooperative and disagreeable they really were. The two of them had to be reprimanded.

When she went over to Evelyn's desk, she said quietly, "Evelyn, may I talk to you at my desk for a moment?"

Evelyn was in the middle of a personal business deal which had run well into its second hour. It was now 11:30 a.m. and Evelyn usually went to lunch from 12 noon to 2:30 p.m. In the mornings, she did not sit down at her desk until 9:55 a.m., ignoring the fact that her working hours were from 9 to 5, with an hour for lunch. She looked up at Sheba, very much annoyed.

"What is it?" Evelyn had worked for the County a good many years and had a lot of friends in that office. She wasn't about to be threatened by anything Sheba could do to her. Besides, she had a flourishing motel business outside of the office with most of her customers from County Bureau # 105.

"I'd like to speak to you over at *My* desk." Sheba was bracing herself, preparing to get a lot of static from the woman, she always did.

"Whatever you have to say to me, you can say it right here. Why should I get up from my chair and go over to your desk?"

Sheba bit her tongue to stop herself from making a cruel remark about losing some of the three hundred pounds Evelyn was carrying around so that she could get up off her chair to do something besides eat. Instead, she said to the staff member at the desk, "Would you mind leaving? I have to speak to Evelyn privately."

The man got up and left without a word.

"Evelyn, I *have* to speak to you. You are supposed to be at your desk at 9 o'clock, but the earliest you arrive at work is 9:30. Still you are not ready to start work. You bring in coffee and cake and proceed to eat your breakfast. By the time you have finished eating, it's break time, which you take from 10:30 to 11:30. Then you go to lunch from noon to 2:30. Right now we have a load of clients and a tremendous amount of backlog waiting to be worked off…"

Evelyn cut into Sheba's last words, snarling.

"Don't blame me, I do my work."

"Not nearly enough, and everything you do has so many errors, I'm constantly sending your work back to you. In addition, I need you here to interview clients, one thing you can do well."

"You are always picking on me. Why? Who do you think you are? Since they kicked your ass out of the office manager's section, you think you are going to take everything out on me. You frustrated bi…

actress. I'm not going to take any shit off you. You come down here trying to change everything, acting like Hitler."

"In other words," Sheba responded "To try to get a days work out of you I need to act like Hitler?"

Evelyn refused to answer. She shifted her huge body on the chair and turned her back to Sheba.

After that, Evelyn didn't bring her personal business to her desk. She just stayed away from her desk, saying that she was in the accounting or statistical sections, and proceeded to take care of her motel business elsewhere.

All Sheba could do at that point was to take up the matter with her supervisor, who in turn would discuss it with Evelyn. Her frustration with this situation was mounting.

The other dissenting worker, Pearl, kept working hours as loose as Evelyn's. She constantly stayed on the telephone, making Sheba think that she had no phone at home. Sometimes her calls would last as long as three hours, while she made a pretense of working. It took Pearl all afternoon to fill out one 3x5 card, with only the name and address of a client. Her track record for speed at work was zilch.

When Sheba spoke to Pearl, she did not get as much flack. Pearl did not like to make a vulgar scene in front of the men on staff.

Thank GOD for little things, Sheba was thinking, as both her delinquent workers miraculously returned from lunch on time.

Pearl sat sullenly down at her desk and stared across the office at the closed door to the back room.

The men wanted to speak to Rafael, who was one of the players.

Meanwhile, in the back, the men sat around the table playing poker. Besides the table and chairs they sat on, the room had a cot. The cot had a notorious reputation for being used for other activities than the first aid for which it was originally intended.

"Hell man, you must'a laid at least 20 different women around here." Drew Baker, a short, stocky Black man said this with a cigar hanging out of the side of his mouth and both elbows on the table.

"Yeah, but Sheba is different." Rafael replied.

"What's so different about that broad, man? As far as I can see, she got tits and ass, just like all the rest of those broads. No different from your wife, man, so get yourself together. Go home and screw your wife. She has the very same fixings that Sheba has." Baker said sharply.

Rafael scowled at Baker. "Shit, man, you ain't got no class."

Baker became furious at this remark. No one could tell him that he was not the epitome of aristocracy and class.

He and his wife earned a total of fifty thousand dollars annually before taxes. They were both college grads, she taught school while he worked for the county as a social caseworker.

Because of high living, he and his wife couldn't save a dime.

Baker's house "out on the island" was a four bedroom elegantly furnished home. His two children lived better than a millionaire's children. Both boys had expensive motorbikes, attended private schools and wore the best clothes money could buy.

"Live for today is my motto." He constantly bragged about his home and furnishings and, as a result, his home had been robbed several times.

He liked to think that he looked like a Black professor, but he had allowed himself to over indulge in too much of the soft life. In addition to wine, women and song, he ate too much of everything. His friends called themselves "swingers" and they drank heavily. Someone in his clique gave a party every weekend. These parties lasted from Friday night until Sunday morning.

Now, still furious, he said to Rafael, "Class, ass. What's the difference?" Baker felt he had plenty of class. Rafael would not know what class was, even if it smacked him in the face. "You just want *everything* for yourself. You can't let any ass pass you up. *You* are a greedy man. Maybe you don't know this, but that broad don't want *you*. I don't know what she wants, but I do know, it ain't you.I can't see getting up in a sweat over nothing. She's a good looking broad, but there are lots of goodlooking broads around here."

He looked at Rafael to see his reaction. Rafael leaned back in his chair, so Baker went on talking.

"Take Shirley, f'instance, that big ass and bunch of tits could have me any day of the week.But I ain't gonna get upset over her, no sir."

The other men looked at Rafael, some of them agreeing silently that Rafael was a greedy man. Carlos didn't say anything because he wanted Sheba himself.

Rafael glared at Baker and said, "You are the jackass. I laid Shirley and that big ass don't screw any better'n anybody else's."

Baker flared up.

"You're a liar. You never screwed Shirley."

"Like I said, *you* are a jackass."

All of the other men laughed.

Baker looked around the table, still angry, but there was nothing he could do about it. Rafael was a foot taller and very muscular. He was quite capable of smashing Baker into little pieces.

He brooded but said nothing else. He had been after Shirley for a long time. She acted as though she was too good to screw him or anybody else. Now, much to his embarrassment, he discovers that tramp has gone to bed with that male whore, Rafael. That hurt him. Maybe Rafael was just bragging, then again, maybe he was lying, trying to impress the other guys.

Baker leaned back in his chair pretending to give thought to the cards in his hands, but he was really giving thought to Rafael.

The big bastard! He tried to lay every woman in County Bureau #105. Short, tall, ugly, beautiful, young or old. He was so damned horny, he would probably go with the men if he could. It infuriated Baker to think that Shirley chose Rafael, a Security Guard, over *him*.

Baker's object of affection, Shirley Oranger, was a pretty Black woman with very smooth brown skin. With the help of every female cosmetic on the market, she spent two hours each morning making herself positively gorgeous. Evelyn and Pearl claimed that in order to be able to paint her face like that, Shirley must be some great artist. They added that she would probably be unrecognizable without all that makeup.

She attracted the attention of the men and of course, made a lot of the women jealous. Her clothes were outstanding, obviously expensive and they were endless. It seemed that every day Shirley wore something new and elaborate.

She had three small children who stayed all week with her mother, and had a flourishing business as a hooker. The other workers wondered how she did it. Then Pearl found out on the newly installed computers that Shirley was also getting welfare and all hell broke loose.

Shirley had turned tricks with several of the men around the office, using Evelyn's motel. Even though she was relatively discreet about her affairs, somebody else talked and Pearl was eager to listen. One of the men who paid for services thought that she overcharged and wasn't worth the price.

She could care less about what he thought and threatened to call his wife if he did not pay.

When Pearl approached her in the lunchroom about being on welfare and being a whore, every jealous woman there jumped on Shirley. She ran from the room in tears, grabbing her bag. She was done with County Bureau #105.

As for Rafael, it was amazing to anyone that really knew him that he would even have the slightest knowledge of the word "class"

Clearly, from his daily encounters, he was not used to decent or respectable women. He was so used to having them fall right into line with what ever he wanted that he did not begin to know how to approach Sheba.

The first day he worked at County Bureau #105 on loan from another location, he met her going into the building.

"Where do you work?" Rafael questioned.

Sheba turned, looked at him without answering and kept right on going. She made him feel a little edgy.

"I'll be working here, starting today. I was wondering if I would be working with you." He wanted to get to know her.

"Oh. I work on the first floor, in the ABD unit." Her face was more relaxed.

There was something about her, not just her looks, that drew him. He glanced down at her legs out of habit, licked his lips lewdly.

His look repulsed her. Slimy come-ons were not her style. Ironically, Rafael thought he was giving her his best romantic "gaze". In truth, he was coming across as a lecherous fool.

"What do you do?" he asked.

"Just about everything."

"Everything?" He leered.

"Look, when I said everything, that only included my legitimate work for the county."

She was cool and unsmiling. He wondered if he would ever learn when to keep quiet. Unconsciously, he reached out to touch her, but she dodged his hand and went into the building.

"Shit." He thought, "I did it again."

Rafael dropped his cigarette to the ground and stepped on it to extinguish the flame. He'd put his foot in his mouth twice. And on his first day.

1954

Sanga Mara-Rafael Cruz's Home Town

Rafael Cruz began consorting with woman at the tender age of 14. His mother and father had stills in the backyard that supplied all the whiskey in the little town of Sanga Mara including the local police force. When his mother and father were out making deliveries, he would sell whiskey to their customers.

The day he first met Elena, the temperature was one hundred and two degrees. It was steaming in Sanga Mara, and you could actually see the heat rising from the ground. The sun was blinding. Rafael had just poured water from the well all over his body and was rubbing himself dry when he looked up and saw Elena, the town whore, watching him.

Everybody, including little children, was aware that Elena was the town whore and drunk. There wasn't a man in Sanga Mara, except perhaps the priest who hadn't shared Elena's dwindling charms.

He wasn't ashamed of his body and when he saw her standing there he grinned at her. She smiled seductively back at him then took his hand and led him into the little room where all the sleeping mats were. Elena was very gentle with him because of his youth, but did not spare him any of her tricks.

That afternoon, Rafael learned every carnal act that Elena knew and some that they created together.

When they were spent, Rafael told her bluntly she would have to get out before his parents came home. It was getting dark and his father would severely whip him if he knew what had taken place.

She left, but not before she talked Rafael out of a very large jug of whiskey, saying she needed it to help her get through the night. After that first time, she would often sneak over there once she saw his parents leave.

As he grew older, he began to take on a variety of women. His ego made him approach older, married women, surprised, at first, that they'd accept his offer.

Sometimes he would wait to see what married man would go into Elena's house, then he would go to the man's wife and avail himself. His reputation for making torrid love was well known among the married women. He was rarely, if ever, turned away.

The single girls, though they were ready and willing, were not considered as able or as knowledgeable as the married women, according to Rafael. Besides, he did not want to make any illegitimate babies. The fathers of Sanga Mara's fair maidens would force him to marry at the business end of a sawed off shotgun.

At age 19, Rafael tired of Sanga Mara and its women. He needed a greater variety and Florida was his preferred destination. The women there were willing, but an angry Black man caught him flirting with his woman. The man told Rafael that he just might get a bullet in the back if he messed around with any of the women there.

A word to the wise is sufficient. Rafael worked there just long enough to make enough money to move on. Even though he picked up a few floosies here and there, his sexual appetite was far from satisfied.

Because of his inner needs, Rafael did not stop until he reached Mega City. On arriving there, he looked the city over and decided this was his meat and potatoes. There were women everywhere, all sizes, shapes, colors and ages.

He met his wife, Nellie, at the first job he got. She was one of several women Rafael was seeing. They got careless, she got pregnant, they got married.

Being married didn't stop Rafael, he was like a steamroller, plowing his way through an army of lonely and frustrated women. County Bureau #105 was no different. Some women had men who were abusing them, others were just waiting for somebody like him to come into their lives.

Right now, poker game over, as he and Carlos stood with their backs to the wall and watched Sheba working hard at her desk, one of the women whom Rafael was going with walked over to talk to Rafael.

Not wanting to over hear their conversation, Carlos walked over to another spot where he could still watch Sheba. He knew that there wasn't any man currently at County Bureau #105 that would really interest Sheba, either they were married or too young. Besides, whenever he had any conversation with her, she indicated she practiced abstinence.

Once he asked her if she had anybody.

"What do you mean? I'm divorced, you know that." she replied.

"You know what I mean. You are all woman and you need a man to make love to you." Carlos said.

She looked at him and replied coolly, "Not without benefit of clergy, I don't."

"You mean you won't make love to any man unless you are married to him?" Carlos was shocked and disappointed.

"That's absolutely correct." Sheba's voice was firm.

"But why deny yourself?" Carlos could not hide the disappointment in his voice.

"Deny myself? You speak from a man's point of view. The next thing you 'll tell me is that I will go crazy from lack of sex."

"Well, it's true. What are you waiting for?" Carlos demanded to know.

"For the very same reasons you married your wife, I suppose. I am one of those rare people you meet who must be in love with the person I mate with, and that man must be in love with me. I'm not a female garbage pail for anybody."

"That's the first time I have ever heard that one. What do you do when you get those warm feelings?"

Sheba thought a while, then against her better judgement explained. "When I'm at work, I work. At home, I have so many things to do, I don't have time to sit and think about those warm feelings."

"What about when you dream at night?" Carlos seemed really bewildered.

"Carlos, what most people need to understand is that it is all in the mind. If you fantasize during your awake hours, sometimes that will dominate your subconcious mind when you are sleeping. I am very much aware of the things I say and do during the day so that I don't often have erotic dreams.When I do it's usually with my ex-husband since he's the only man I've been intimate with. Does that satisfy you?"

He gazed at her dreamily, thinking about the dreams *he* had about *her*. After this conversation, she stayed on his mind. He wondered what made him think of this Black woman so often. He tried hard to forget her, but the more he tried to forget her, the more she haunted his thoughts. Yet his wife and children really mattered to him.

He understood where Sheba was coming from because of his own strict Italian backround. His parents taught him decent values, which of course included the church, even though he came from one of the toughest neighborhoods in Mega City.

He gained himself an early reputation. Although he was only five foot seven, Carlos was quite muscular. The girls chased him shamelessly, loving his dark, good looks and fine physique. He never seduced any girl, letting *them* make all the overtures. Nice girls never looked for trouble, his father told him in a man-to-man talk. His father also told him he'd better not have any babies without being married or else he would have to marry the girl. So, Carlos managed to restrain himself until his fifteenth birthday.

On that day, Carlos was on the roof of the tenement house cooling off. The weather was very hot and muggy. He heard a step behind him and turned around, it was Peggy Krasner, the wife of Irving Krasner, who owned a little grocery store three blocks away. The Krasners lived in Carlos' building.

Peggy looked greedily at Carlos, who's shirt was laying nearby. Carlos' shoulders were very wide and her eyes were glued to his body.

She only had on a flimsy robe and it was not tied together very well. When she walked toward Carlos, the belt became untied and the robe fell open. There was nothing underneath.

Peggy pressed her body to Carlos' and he stood frozen to the spot, a flushed feeling overwhelming him. At first, he was quite embarrassed, but his embarrassment soon disappeared when she kissed him first on the cheeks ever so gently, then full on the lips.

Her body was warm and soft, and she knew how to turn him on to her. It was an experience that Carlos never forgot.

He never told anybody, especially not his friends.

That's why he respected Sheba, There weren't too many women or girls who carried themselves like her or respected themselves. Maybe, and he laughed to himself, maybe that was why he felt he wanted her so much. Other women chased him, he wasn't bad looking. He was prematurely gray and still very handsome. His personality was pleasant to both men and women. If he could comply with anybody's request for a favor, he did not refuse.

Happily married for over 20 years, he had four children, the youngest 16. His wife Patricia was beautiful even after all those years, she took good care of herself. She worked too. Together they made a comfortable living. Patricia, worked daily as a barmaid for a chic bar in the suburbs. Because she was so attractive and shapely, her tips were generous, bringing home three and four hundred dollars per week. Half of this she threw in a dresser drawer so that anytime either of them needed money, it was there. The other half went into a savings account. Carlos paid all the bills out of his salary.

They got along beautifully and Carlos did not want that to change. Until he met Sheba, there wasn't anybody he wanted to make love to other than his wife.

But from the first moment he saw her, he wanted her. According to the so-called experts, she might not be considered beautiful. But according to Carlos, she was as beautiful as a woman could be. Sheba had a special aura about her, an intense radiation of personality that reached out positively to most men and women.

Carlos thought the feelings he had for her would wear off after awhile, since he was still very much in love with his wife.But the more he saw her, the more he thought about her. He let her know many times he was interested, but she never took the bait. She knew he was a married man and told him that as far as she was concerned, married men were strictly off limits and not fair game. She laughed and joked with him but did not stand for any vulgarities.

Once he got out of line and she did not speak to him for two weeks, and then only after he apologized profusely to her. He was surprised at himself that he cared so much for her approval.

After that incident, he treated Sheba with greater respect than he had for any woman, including his mother. She softened a little toward him. Once, when he passed her in the hall, he took her hand tenderly and squeezed it gently and said "I love you."

Sheba smiled back and answered, "I love you too," and kept on walking.

His heart skipped a beat as he walked on, too. The magnetism between the two was undeniable.

Sheba suspected that Carlos cared for her, but she wasn't about to fool herself and become romantically entangled in an affair that could not possibly go anywhere. Liking him, she sympathized with his occasional small displays of affection for her as long as he did not get carried away.

He was standing by her desk when Rafael came over and jokingly warned her about Carlos.

"I know Carlos, he is completely harmless." Laughing, Rafael repeated this for Carlos' benefit.

Harmless, hell! What could he do about Sheba? Carlos was becoming frustrated and felt that if he did not do something he would crack up. Finally he decided to leave County Bureau #105 and work elsewhere. He requested and got a transfer to another County Agency.

****

Paul McDonald, one of the young men whom Pearl gossiped to be Sheba's lover, watched Sheba step off the elevator and move toward her desk. He waited for her to sit down before he approached her.

Paul was just 20 years old and the best-looking man in the office. His looks were both an asset and a liability. The girls and women chased him like mad. At first, when he came to County Bureau #105, he was amazed at how easy it was to twist them around his little finger.

All except Sheba and he really dug Sheba. She could twist him around *her* little finger anytime.

Sometimes he sat at his desk and surveyed the office around him. What a bunch of floosies! All the young chicks looked like hell burned out. They looked as worn as some of the old, used up hags there who tried to flirt with him, such as Pearl.

Sheba was plenty of years older than Paul, but sometimes she could almost pass for his age. In fact, when he first met her, he thought she was his age and he fell hard.Then Pearl found out how he felt about Sheba, and told him that she was in her 30's.

Paul was shocked initially, he did not believe that Pearl was telling the truth. But he asked one of the men who'd known her longer than he did, and was told that the divorced Sheba had a 13 year old daughter.

After the shock wore off, it didn't make any difference to him. He couldn't help himself anymore, he was in deep water. No matter what they said about her, or how hard they teased him, he still was pretty much sure he loved her.

"In 20 years when you are still young," Pearl said slyly, "She will be an old woman and ugly."

"You must be at least 50 years old yourself, and you're not so old and ugly." Paul answered her.

Pearl fancied herself a young-looking sexpot. She was barely 30 years old, and she was moderately attractive. Paul usually teased her about her age. He did this because she was so jealous of Sheba that she constantly made vicious and cruel remarks about her to Paul, trying to change the way he felt.

What she or anyone else said about Sheba wasn't going to turn his feelings off.

Sheba had never paid any special attention to him in the two years he'd worked there. In many ways, he tried to let her know how he felt about her, but she would not let on that she knew. Paul was getting damned frustrated.

He couldn't know that Sheba knew and was drawn to him, but the age difference was too great. He was only 7 years older than her daughter, she couldn't imagine Donna calling him daddy.

But Paul didn't reason that way. He was beginning to think that it was his salary. He was a junior clerk, she was a Administrative Assistant earning almost twice his salary. No way he could compete with that.

He was one of several now watching Sheba as she worked at her desk. Rafael, the greedy man, and Carlos were both staring in Sheba's direction.

Remembering his dream of the night before, holding her body close to him, the thought made tremors shoot through his body all over again.He turned and walked swiftly to the men's room. Damn it she was driving him up the wall.

When he came back, she was gone, his spirits sank.

For want of something to do, other than the filing that was stacked up on the file cabinets, he walked over to Emmy Lou and started teasing her.Emmy Lou had a deep crush on Paul. He tried to stay there until Sheba returned to her desk, hoping she would get jealous.

"Paul," Emmy Lou drawled in a heavy southern accent, "If you don't get away from heah, y'all gonna' be sorry." She was a tiny, shapely girl, whose short, straight black hair blended in with her skin.

Wishing he'd stay, she watched him spitefully turn and walk away from her desk.

He went to his desk to wait until Sheba came back. Pearl was sitting at her desk, which was next to Paul's. Sometimes he couldn't stand her, but she was a good listener. She'd sit for long lengths of time, listening to him talk about Sheba and pretending to understand. He seemed to be unaware of how much Pearl hated Sheba and the extent of her jealousy.

"Emmy Lou is a very nice girl, why don't you take her out?" Pearl asked as sweetly as she could manage.

"Her hair is too short." Paul answered.

"That's no reason, are you prejudiced against girls with short hair, Paul? I have short hair, wouldn't you take me out?"

"I wouldn't go anywhere with you Pearl." Paul's voice was abrupt but Pearl ignored this and kept plowing on.

"Take me to the Black Rodeo, Paul. I'll even pay for the tickets."

"I just told you, I wouldn't go anywhere with you. Ask your husband to take you."

"He's working."

"So am I."

"I mean, at night."

"So tell him to take the night off."

"What! And lose all that money?"

"I'll take Sheba."

"She's too old for you."

"So are you, in fact, you're older than she is."

"No. She is older than I am."

"You look older than Sheba and that's what counts."

Just then, Sheba reappeared, getting Paul's full attention. Pearl's huge eyes, which were emphasized with thick, black eyeliner pencil, stared at Sheba with hate.

When Sheba sat down at her desk, Paul said to Pearl, "I'd marry Sheba next week if she would let me."

Pearl rolling her eyes replied, "I'll buy you a beautiful wedding gift if she marries you."

"Oh yeah? It's a deal."

Pearl continued to glare over at Sheba with malice on her face. Paul was too busy looking at Sheba to notice. His mind was on the curve of her lips, which he possessed every night in his dreams while making imaginary love to her. It seemed as though they were married already.

His thoughts drifted back to reality and the time they were both waiting for the elevator. He had walked over to Sheba and held her in his arms tenderly. She didn't resist and he became aroused.

"I'm hot, aren't you?" he whispered to Sheba.

She said, "Take that sweater off."

"You know what I mean," he answered.

She smiled at him, turned and entered the elevator.

The next afternoon, he came up behind her and murmured in her ear, "How about a date?"

She answered, "Okay."

Sheba had been talking to Pearl and Vera, when Paul came over to her. Both of the women heard Paul ask her out.

"When?" he asked a little louder.

The women looked at Sheba expectantly. Sheba, noting the expressions on their faces, did not answer

Paul, but squeezed his hand, hoping he would understand.

But Paul didn't understand. He thought that she did not answer him because she did not want to go out with him and he became angry. He walked away hurt, not realizing that he had made his move at the worst possible time. Pearl and Vera were two of County Bureau #105's most vicious gossips. They were just waiting to get something on Sheba. Pearl saw Sheba squeeze Paul's hand and that was all she needed to get started on some hot gossip. She couldn't wait to lay this on the women in the lunch room.

From that day forward, Pearl's campaign against Sheba heightened. Paul listened. Though he was sure he loved Sheba, he was hurt because she was not displaying any open affection for him like some of the other women did. If she liked him, why didn't she acknowledge him?

He was confused, nothing he did seemed to reach her.

To make matters worse, he was also jealous of his good friend, Antonio. Pearl told him that Sheba was in love with Antonio. That was the day Antonio gave Sheba a necklace he had hand crafted out of spent rifle shells from his family's property in Puerto Rico where they hunted wild game.

Paul couldn't make anything like that, but he would do anything else she asked him to do. Anything, including buying her expensive gifts.

Loudly, Pearl would declare to anyone who would listen, "Sheba should leave these young boys alone." Once after stating that loudly, she put her arms around him and kissed him full on the lips. This she considered perfectly innocent and beyond any kind of negative judgement, but all Paul had to do was look at Sheba or compliment her and Sheba would again fall victim to Pearl's viper tongue.

Events were to come that proved Paul very capable of operating on his own, stunning everyone at County Bureau # 105, including Sheba *and* Pearl.

A temporary new Center Director was sent in to cover the location when the old director retired. The new director was a woman, Agatha Fluddrucker, with the civil service title of Supervising Caseworker.

After six months in the director's position, she was proving to be more irritating than helpful to employees. Mrs. Fluddrucker favored certain employees and others she leaned on hard. The patrolmen disliked her for stopping the card games in the back room, ordering that that door be kept open at all times.

One Jewish holiday, staff was scarce, but miraculously, very few clients came into the center that day. Many of the managerial staff took the day off and Sheba was next in line for duty after the director.

About three o'clock in the afternoon, Agatha's secretary came rushing into Sheba's office.

"Mrs. Welters, there's something wrong with the director."

Gwendolyn looked very distressed. She was the only one who Agatha treated like a human being because of her dependency upon the secretary for privacy and confidentiality on many important and private matters.

"What happened?" Sheba asked, rising from her chair on the way to help even before Gwendolyn could answer her.

"Well, a very important phone call came in from the Field Director, Mr. Schwartzenegger, at central office. I buzzed Mrs. Fluddruckers's line, but she didn't answer. I tried again, three or four times, and still no answer. Then I tried the door and it's locked. I dont have a key to her office."

The woman was so upset, Sheba felt sorry for her. "And I know she hasn't left!"

"All right! First I'll call Omarr and the patrolmen and have them meet us at her office door. Then we'll go straight there. Maybe she fell asleep at her desk." Sheba made the call but in truth, she couldn't imagine Agatha, who was usually hyper, falling asleep at her desk for any reason. She was just trying to calm Gwendolyn. There wasn't much sense in speculating, they'd soon find out what had happened.

Omarr and Rafael were waiting at Agatha's door when Sheba and Gwendolyn arrived. Rafael knocked loudly on the door several times, then took the keys from Omarr when there was no answer. He opened the door and went in, while Sheba, Omarr and Gwendolyn followed.

"Well, I'll be damned!" murmured Omarr, the custodian. His mouth was so close to Sheba's ear that the heat from his heavy breathing on her neck made her shudder. She stared in horror and disgust at the two writhing bodies on the director's conference table. Turning to get away, she found Omarr's hulking body blocking her way. He was luridly fascinated by the scene before them, completely forgetting Sheba's presence.

"Move out of my way." Sheba's voice was suddenly quite cold.

His huge frame moved only enough to allow her to squeeze by him. He didn't want to miss anything.

Sheba made tracks for her own desk. She couldn't get away from there fast enough. Her destination was a cubicle in the ladies room to be alone.

Once there, she recapitulated in her mind the events leading to that bizarre discovery. She could not believe what she had seen with her own eyes. It seemed too unreal. Maybe it was because she did not want to believe what she saw. It was ghastly and ludicrous. Paul McDonald and Agatha Fluddrucker! She, of all people, to witness that horrible scene. What really hurt and devastated her more than anything else was that she was just beginning to trust Paul.

He was a really great hunk of a Black man and had almost convinced Sheba that his affection for her was genuine. Paul took great pleasure in doing things for her, fixing her car, painting her apartment, etc. When she tried to pay him, he was really insulted.

Then, when his mother gave a barbeque, he invited Sheba and Donna.

They enjoyed themselves there and were treated with respect by his mother and other relatives, much to Sheba's surprise. Paul had not invited anyone else from County Bureau #105 and neither of them mentioned the outing to their co-workers. Sheba was beginning to be comfortable with him. She thought maybe she now could accept going out with him on a real date.

But now, in the ladies room, Sheba closed the door behind her and locked it. Leaning against the door she cried silently. And let the tears flow until she blistered her eyes.

Of all the women in the place for him to become involved with. Agatha Fluddrucker had a notorious reputation even before she came to County Bureau #105. She was White, with large, bulging, evil eyes in a face surrounded by long, stringy, red hair that reached her buttocks when it was loose. It was usually worn in a bun on top of her head. She bore a strong resemblance to the "Wicked Witch of the West", and behaved in the same fashion. She was dubbed "Ms. Bitch" behind her back, for her cruel and sadistic treatment of staff, peers and the world at large, family and friends included.

Agatha's ruddy complexion made her look constantly flushed with purple veins from her temples to her jaws. She was only four foot eleven and quite scrawny, but rumor had it that she had once weighed over three hundred pounds. A diet of black coffee and cigarettes helped shed most of the excessive fat and flab. She received so many compliments on her weight loss, that now she pictured herself as beautiful and irresistible.

Hence, today's happening.

Agatha had stalked Paul with a vengeance. It did not matter that she was married, her marriage meant nothing to her. Prior to Paul, it was rumored that she had had a female lover who commited suicide because of her slashing her own wrists.

The death of her lover, the director at another County Bureau site, who had been influential in helping Agatha get her current position as director seemed to have no outward affect on Agatha. She coldly announced the woman's demise at a meeting of the administrative staff. There were a few furtive glances around the table, but no one dared utter a word or comment. The news was, in fact, old hat by then. Agatha was trying to make staff believe that the woman did not mean anything to her. She told herself that her staff would believe anything she told them, especially since 90% of her staff was Black and she was White.

The dead woman, Ida Rifkin, was also small and extremely thin, but quite masculine in appearance. She had worn women's clothing, mostly pants and tailored blouses, and still managed to resemble a man in female apparel. Her hair was medium length and hung limp and uncurled. A little brown cigar was always hanging out of the side of her mouth. As a director she was a tyrant and dominated her location like Simon Legree.

Under no circumstances did she change her mind about anything. Not even when she was dead wrong. A trait that Agatha picked up from her.

When Ida learned that Agatha was seeing a Black man, she waited until they were in bed before she confronted her. Agatha in one of her more vicious moods, snarled at Ida, "Yes. I play games with a Black man and he's a far better lover than you are."

Ida rolled away from her and started to froth around the mouth. "You filthy slut! Get out of here! I dont want to see you around here again!"

Agatha laid back on the bed, put her hands behind her head and crossed her legs.

Shrieking at the top of her lungs, Ida repeated, "Get the hell out of here, you slut!" Realizing that Agatha wasn't going anywhere, she ran out of the room and returned with a 45 handgun.

"Get out of here, you slut." Ida aimed the gun at Agatha.

"You won't shoot." Agatha said coolly, rolling over. Her nude body gleamed from the light of the table lamp. She spread her legs in a vulgar position and laughed.

Ida cocked the gun and pulled the trigger. The gun exploded and the bullet went into the bed between Agatha's legs. She stopped laughing and started screaming. Agatha leapt up and ran, and did stop running until she was six blocks away from Ida's apartment. Her floppy breasts were beating against her ribs as she ran. Until that moment, she'd been unaware of how much flab she still had on her body. Exposed to the world, she felt like a bowl of gelatin.

Two hours later, accompanied by two patrolman and wearing a borrowed coat, she returned to the apartment. Outside were several police cars and a station wagon from the coroner's office.

One of the patrolmen with Agatha approached an officer already on the scene.

"What happened here?"

"A woman committed suicide." he answered coolly.

The patrolman with Agatha explained why he was there and was told that Ida must have committed suicide right after Agatha fled from the apartment. They started whispering after that, watching Agatha from the corner of their eyes.

Officer Dart came back to Agatha speaking low and sympathetically to her.

"I'm afraid I have bad news for you."

Her eyebrows shot up.

"Your friend committed suicide." Agatha looked relieved. At least she didn't have to worry about Ida coming after her with that big gun anymore.

Agatha Fluddrucker and Paul McDonald were transferred out of County Bureau #105, to different sites. Agatha was demoted back to Supervising Caseworker. Paul's title couldn't get any lower, but he was exiled to a very lonely stockroom. He eventually quit that job and became a police officer.

****

Shortly after Paul left County Bureau #105, Sheba's unit got a new welfare client, Alfred Q. Greene.

Alfred was really a very intelligent man, 30 years old and bordering on the brink of genius. Presently, he was under treatment at a mental clinic as an out patient, having just recently been released from an institution.

Despite his brilliance, he had not been accepted at any of the corporations to which he applied for work, knowing it was because he was Black.

He was a well-traveled man and had loved living abroad, coming back to the United States out of sheer necessity.

His hatred toward the American government because of being treated so badly, drove him insane. Suddenly, he began talking to himself, ranting against the U.S.A. at all hours of the day and night, everywhere and anywhere. He did not care where he initiated his tirades, he had completely lost control of himself.

Finally, when he went into a crowded department store and began shouting to the people, security grabbed him and had him taken away. But not before the arrival of about twenty policemen and an ambulance with orderlies to straightjacket him. He was taken to a mental hospital for observation.

When they found out that he was an armed forces' veteran, they shipped him to a veterans' hospital. They subjected him to all kinds of psychiatric tests, including a scan which searched for brain tumors. His very complex mind believed that the doctors were inserting some kind of transistorized computer in his head. Electrodes were attached to his head and body while the scan was taking place.

He stayed in the hospital for six months. When he was released, he took to drinking to try and stop the noises in his head. Alfred suffered under the belief that the scanner was still inside his head so the government could spy on him.

Alfred believed the government inserted the scanner because they did not like his Black looks, firmly believing that the President of the U.S.A., the Governor of the State, and the Mayor of Mega City were all invloved in a sinister plot to sabotage him.

Alfred was also angered at being approached by homosexuals who accused him of being weird because he did not want men. He was extremely proud of his manhood, he had good reason to be. Many women chased Alfred openly, some very beautiful women. His tall, well built physique was like a magnet to most women. In spite of his illness, his looks were cleancut and healthy.

Immediately following his release from the hospital, he made his way to County Bureau #105. His application for assistance was processed swiftly. Yet, he was still unhappy because he felt he was being treated badly by the government.

Because of his disability, his case was transferred to Sheba's unit.

The first time Alfred went into the unit and spotted Sheba, he felt attracted to her. She reminded him of the French girls he had met while studying in Paris under a scholarship. The fact that Sheba was Black made her even more interesting to him.

He was still aggravated though, and gave Sheba and the other workers a hard time. The next time he came in he was furious because they could not find his case record.

Alfred looked for Sheba, she gave him a certain amount of pleasure watching her. After going home that night, he decided that he would try to be nice to her.

The next visit he made to the county office, he noticed she was wearing her hair differently. It was very long and she had it piled in ringlets on top of her head.

"Hello," he called to her.

"Hello, Mr. Greene."

"You look very beautiful. Your hair is in a Parisian hairstyle." He even managed to smile at her when he said this.

This made him momentarily happy, but anger quickly overcame him when he thought that she would probably reject further advances from him. She might not want him for many reasons, especially since he did not have a job.

Maybe if he tried to change himself, she would want him. He would try to be what she wanted. He couldn't wait for his next trip to the County Bureau to get his check and see Sheba.

On his next visit, he was clean shaven, the beard and mustache gone, looking years younger. When Sheba saw him from a distance, she was pleasantly surprised again. She almost did not recongnize him.

Upon close scrutiny though, she was surprised again. Alfred Q. Greene had pierced a hole in his nose and had a toothpick in the hole extending out of the nostril. He had also pierced each ear lobe once and had strings in the holes to keep them open.

This day, Alfred was prepared to actually try to get Sheba to go out with him. He had dreamed about her more than once. It was a while since he had dreamed about any woman. It was always that scanner he dreamed about.

Alfred recalled the day he asked her if she were Miss or Mrs.

"I'm Ms." she replied.

"Oh. One of those." But he assumed from that that she was not married. He was happy.

Sheba now was in the process of searching for his case record, which was missing again. Alfred waited impatiently for Sheba to return. He wanted to see her and wondered what took her so long.

He had heard her tell one of the workers she would be on the fourth floor. Alfred decided he would go up there and check Sheba out.

As he got off the elevator, he could hear Sheba's voice coming from somewhere and he followed the sound.

"You can't miss him, he has a gray knit hat on, a toothpick sticking out of his nose and pierced ears with training strings in them."

Alfred walked into the room where Sheba was sitting. When she saw him she was startled, but she managed to keep her cool, and he decided to keep his.

Firmly, she said, "Mr. Greene, you aren't supposed to be on this floor."

"I know that, but I want to know what's happening with my check."

"We are doing our very best to locate your records."

"Why is something always happening with *my* records? Is it the government again?"

Sheba looked at him puzzled. Alfred went on to explain.

"You see, the government has it in for me."

"Why?"

"They don't like my looks."

"That doesn't mean they come in here and steal your records." Sheba answered uneasily.

"Oh yes. They've done much worse. They are the ones that drove me out of my mind. They put a scanner inside my head and it makes noises. I took to drinking large amounts of alcohol to try to drive the noises out of my head." Alfred wasn't angry yet but he was slowly getting there.

"Just because they don't like your looks, you think the government did all of that to you? They would kill you first."

"They *were* trying to kill me."

Alfred's voice was getting louder and louder. The staff nearby were staring at him, not knowing whether to call the patrolman or not.

"Well, Mr. Greene, I think it would be cheaper for the government to eliminate you with a bullet, rather than to go to all of that trouble. Is the scanner still in your head?"

"No. They came one night while I was sleeping at home and took it out. Too many people knew about it, so they had to get rid of it. The president, the Governor and the Mayor all had something to do with it. The President even wrote it up in a report."

"I probably could believe that if you had another reason. But to do all that to you just because somebody does not like your looks, sounds very unreasonable."

He looked at Sheba for a few minutes.

If he could just read her mind. There was no expression on her face. He couldn't tell if she was laughing at him.

"You know, I've been all over Europe and I'm going back there. In fact, I'm going to see about my passport this afternoon. You may not see me here any more. I can't take living in this country."

Sheba thought, then said "So you think Europe is better?"

"I know it is. My friends are there, I'll have a place to stay. Living is much cheaper."

"How will you manage? Will you work?"

"Eventually. But my friends will care for me until then. Maybe I'll come back and drop a bomb on this country."

"You wouldn't do that. Think of all the innocent people you would hurt, people who are in the same situation that you are."

"It's just a thought. I didn't make any definite plans."

"I'm glad to hear that. Well, I'd better get back to work so that you can get your check."

She jumped up from the desk and Alfred's eyes followed her around the room. His head turned like a swivel each time she walked to a different section in the office.

Finally, she walked over to him and said, "I'll have to go to another floor."

"I'll follow you."

"You're supposed to wait downstairs."

"I know, but where you go, I go." He hesitated, then asked, "maybe I could take you for a steak dinner."

Sheba shrugged her shoulders and went to the floor below. After a few minutes, she gave up the search and went back to her unit.

She gave instructions to create a dummy record and issue Alfred his check. In half an hour, Alfred had his check in his hand and was on his way. He did not remember until too late that Sheba did not give him an answer on his steak offer.

****

Sheba's immediate supervisor was Yetta Nenner, a good-looking White woman in her late forties. She had a youthful appearance and was usually good natured when not working. When she was working, she felt she was compelled to show her authority by being tough.

Yetta rose swiftly through the ranks because she was a close friend of the office manager and she did not mind cutting a few throats or sleeping around to get what she wanted. After being a housewife until her children were grown and married, she started working with the county as a clerk. In five years, she rose to the provisional position of Administrative Associate, the position she now held, and received a fat paycheck every two weeks. Her husband also brought home a fat paycheck from the bakery where he was head baker. Between the two of them they brought home enough money to be able to afford an eighty thousand dollar home in the suburbs, and a bank account of over $250,000.00. They traveled whenever they could to get away from their jobs.

Yetta was a chronic flirter, with anybody and everybody, as long as it was a warm male body. None were too old or too young, regardless of race, color or creed. She liked feeling good and it made her feel good to flirt and get a positive response.

She admired Sheba for her brains and her looks. Yetta figured she did not have to be jealous of Sheba since she felt she was better looking and smarter. After all, she was Sheba's boss.

Still, Yetta was a little wary of Sheba.

Professionally speaking, she and Sheba had the same civil service title, having passed the same City exam. Because of Yetta's friend in management, he appointed her to the higher position on a provisional basis.

Although Yetta was sharp and could pass exams quite well, Sheba always managed to get a higher mark or rating. This placed Sheba way ahead of Yetta on exam lists, which really did not matter because Yetta's friend always kept her ahead of the game. She never got demoted, her salary always went up, never down. People ahead of her on the list got shipped out to *undersirable* locations, but Yetta remained at County Bureau #105 close to her home.

Yetta was constantly polishing apples. The office manager's section was filled with weak-minded people who fed their egos on Yetta's insincere flattery.

Suddenly, Yetta's personal life began to present problems and she changed her attitude toward Sheba. Unfortunately, Yetta began to see Sheba as a threat to her position at County Bureau #105.

Yetta started to undermine Sheba every chance she got. She did nothing openly, but opposed her in subtle ways, thinking Sheba would get transferred elsewhere.

Sheba was an excellent worker, as was her co-worker, Josephine Cannell, who also supervised an ABD unit. The two of them kept their units up-to-date as much as humanly possible. Since those two units were the only units that strictly covered the disabled, Sheba and Josephine had their hands full. Sheba had one less worker than Josephine because Central office listed a worker assigned to a satellite site in the suburbs as working in Sheba's unit. Sheba did not benefit from this because the worker did not do her unit's work.

Evelyn and Pearl were reassigned to other sections and two new workers replaced them.

Fortunately, Sheba's current workers cooperated with her and the unit operated effectively.

Yetta had now assigned Sheba an all-Jewish staff. When the Jewish religious holidays came, Sheba had no workers to interview clients, issue checks, accept applications, etc. Sheba telephoned upstairs to request a loan of staff from some of the units that had a full crew. Yetta ignored Sheba's request. That day Sheba interviewed clients and did a lot of the work her four workers normally did.

When Sheba went home that night, she was dead tired and vowed not to go through the same torture she went through that day again.

The next day the same thing happened. Sheba phoned Yetta for staff and was ignored. When Josephine came over to speak to her about something else, she realized, "Sheba, I see you have no workers. What happened?"

"They all stayed out for the holidays." Sheba replied as camly as she could. The stress was really building up in her. Yetta refused to stop the reception area from sending clients to Sheba's unit.

"One of them should have come in."

"Which one?" Sheba asked. She was annoyed with Josephine who had an all Black unit with a crew of five. Sheba expected Josephine to volunteer at least one of her workers to help her interview clients. Josephine was supposed to be her friend, as well as a co-worker. They covered for each other when one of them was absent. In view of this, Sheba said as quietly as possible,"If I don't get at least one worker very soon, I'm going home." Josephine thought she was bluffing. "I am not going to let this job kill me. What about letting me have one of your workers for today?"

"I'm not going to give up any of my workers unless Yetta tells me to."

Sheba was stunned by her answer and her attitude. The woman was almost nasty. They were friends, at least Sheba thought they were, because Josephine had gotten mugged a total of seven times on her way home from work. When they had had an occasion to chat one day, Josephine mentioned this to Sheba. Immediately, Sheba asked her how far she lived from County Bureau #105. It was a nearby address, so Sheba volunteered to drive Josephine home every day.

Sheba thought to herself, 'a friend in need is a friend indeed'.

It was growing close to twelve o'clock. Sheba gave Josephine a disgusted look, and started clearing her desk, preparing to leave.

"Where are you going?" Josephine started to panic.

"Home!" Sheba answered, irritated to the bone.

"Does Yetta know you're going home?" Josephine whined.

"No, and I don't care." Sheba stated bluntly.

"You'd better let her know." Josephine was looking at the large number of clients waiting to be serviced by Sheba's unit. She knew she was going to be stuck with them.

"Why should I?" Sheba was really getting angry now. She had to bite her tongue to keep from giving Josephine a very large and concise piece of her mind. After working her rear end off the day before, without any kind of appreciation or thanks, all Yetta and the office manager expected was that she should do it again. Sheba left.

Back when Sheba and Josephine worked under Yetta, interviewing clients, etc, Yetta depended on the two of them to clean up all the work. The other workers were either just naturally slow or goofed the time away.

When time to evaluate staff came around, Yetta gave everyone a satisfactory performance evaluation, including the goof-offs and incompetents.

Although Sheba and Josephine resented this, there was nothing they could do about it except deliberately slow down. After all why work so hard if the effort was unappreciated?

When promotions came through, Sheba and Josephine to group supervisors, Yetta to assistant office manager, Yetta also became a dictator. The employees hated to go to her for anything. They bypassed her whenever possible or found another AOM to sign work. Sheba suspected Yetta did this because she was not as knowledgeable as she pretended to be. Her mind was not focused on the job.

As the pressures mounted at County Bureau #105, more workers were hired to serve the growing number of welfare recipients, due to an increasing number of unemployed.

One day as Yetta came walking arrogantly down the office aisle between the workers' desks, she looked around at the staff as if to say 'Keep working, you bastards.'

Suddenly, she froze in her tracks.

The blood drained from her face and she turned ashen. Over at the last desk, newly hired by someone above her, sat Ronald Herbert. His head was bent and he was concentrating on his work. Slowly, he lifted his head and his eyes met hers. A smile came over his Black face as he gave her a lustful once-over.

Yetta knew what he was thinking.

Her mind went back five years to when Ronald was 18 years old. He had just started working at County Bureau #105 as a file clerk.

That year, there was a wild Christmas Party, booze flowing like water, and Yetta got staggering drunk. She invited Ronald and five other young Black men into the back room 'to get to know her real well.'

After the fellows had all of her that they wanted, she felt a little guilty. She thought she would balance the books and get a White man in on the deal. Caseworker Harold Stein happened to be nearby, so she called him into the back room.

That Christmas party was vivid in her mind, although she tried very hard to forget it. The Black men involved were either tranferred to different locations or went into the armed forces. Ronald was one of the latter.

Never again did she let anything like that happen, at least not quite that way.

Now, as she stood there mortified, looking at Ronald, she felt so ashamed, she wished the floor would open up and she could disappear.

After that, her world seemed to come tumbling down around her. Her friend in management retired and when she tried to get a transfer out, they refused her request.

To make matters worse, her son Seth was in his mid-twenties and separated from his wife. Seth had gained two hundred pounds since his marriage, going from a husky, well-built one hundred and eighty pounds to an enormous three hundred and eighty-five pounds. He was five foot ten inches tall, and could hardly carry that much weight. It broke Yetta's heart to see her son like that. When his wife and kids left him, Seth had a nervous breakdown.

Yetta had done everything she could do to try to hold that marriage together. She helped them financially to get a private home in the suburbs.

The house only added to their problems. Seth's wife had to stop working because it was impossible for her to commute to work and look after their two children. They couldn't find a satisfactory baby-sitter.

In addition, their sex life was being destroyed because of Seth's obesity. Worst of all, Seth's greed was impossible to live with. As soon as his wife, Marilyn, cooked dinner, there he was, with his big fat hand in the pot.

There were times when he would polish off everything, especially the meats, before Marilyn could fix dinner. She often had to open cans of soup to feed her and the children, sometimes Seth eyed that too.

Marilyn's breaking point came when she cooked dinner early one day so that she could take the children to the pediatrician for a checkup. She left a huge sign on the refrigerator door stating, 'Seth, The children and I did not eat yet. Just leave the small tray of food for us, you take the large tray for yourself.' The large tray had five times the amount of the smaller tray.

She made a mental note before she left, that the freezer was empty, and she would have to shop the next day. The doctor's office was crowded, and

Marilyn and the children did not get home until after eight o'clock. They were all tired and hungry, and she was glad she had dinner waiting.

As Marilyn entered the kitchen, the anger swelled up inside of her. She felt as if she would surely explode like a keg of lit dynamite.

Both trays were empty and the sink was full of dirty dishes waiting for her to wash. This was the last straw! Seth had eaten an entire seven pound roast, four pounds of stringbeans, a bowl of salad, a butter pound cake and a loaf of bread. Two half gallon bottles of soda and a gallon of milk were also missing from the refrigerator.

Tears ran down Marilyn's cheeks as she looked around the devastated kitchen. She felt totally drained and helpless. As she stood there, Seth came waddling into the kitchen and tried to kiss her with his fat repulsive lips.

She slapped his face as hard as she could. The children were sitting there at the table waiting to eat and there was nothing to give them, not even a glass of milk.

Seth knew immediately why Marilyn slapped him.

"I'm sorry, honey, but everything was just so delicious, I couldn't help myself. You sure are some cook... Seth's voice trailed off as Marilyn took the children by the hand and led them out the front door.

Seth was still standing there with his mouth open as Marilyn's car pulled out of the driveway.

He couldn't believe she'd slapped him!

Then he began to get angry. Some nerve she had, slapping him. He was the only one working and it was his money that paid for that food. When she came back home, he was going to give her a piece of his mind, maybe even slap her back.

What Seth did not realize, was that a piece of his mind had already gone with Marilyn.

She and the children did not come back.

He stayed up half the night, waiting for them to return, finally going to bed deciding to be asleep when they came home. Next morning, he went to work brooding. They hadn't come home. He expected Marilyn to be home with the kids when he got there after work with dinner ready and waiting for him to devour as usual.

The house was quiet, and the kitchen empty of food and dirty dishes and pans still in the sink.

Not a drop of food or drink in the house, except for tap water. His appetite had taken care of that the night before. Marilyn had not shopped for him. He missed the ready made meals more than he missed Marilyn and the kids. When he went upstairs to get some petty cash out of Marilyn's dresser drawer so that he could order take-out food, the money was gone. So were Marilyn's and the kids' clothes. She had also taken the joint bank account book and all the important papers with her. He called the bank and confirmed that she had withdrawn all of the savings.

By the time Seth called Yetta, he was already on his way to his nervous breakdown. He was crying on the phone to her because there was no dinner waiting for him when he got home that day. Yetta listened to Seth, biting her tongue. He was trying to make Marilyn the villain, when Yetta knew that she and the kids were the victims of Seth's greedy appetite. Marilyn had discussed the situation with her many times. When they were short of food, Yetta would give Marilyn money to buy groceries. Yetta tried to reason with Seth every chance she got, to try and control his greedy appetite. He simply would not listen.

Yetta told Seth to lock the house up and stay with her and Sam for awhile.She dreaded this, she couldn't stand watching him eat. As a matter of fact, she didn't know how Marilyn had stood him this long.

Seth locked up the house and headed for his mother's home.

He never got there.

His driving was so atrocious in his weakened mental state, that the police stopped him for questioning. They thought he was drunk. His answers were incoherant enough that they took him to a mental institution. The staff there managed to find Yetta's telephone number in his wallet.

After eight months of confinement, Seth improved both mentally and physically. He lost eighty pounds. Even though there was no immediate sign of release, Yetta had hope for him.

Now, she also had her job to worry about in addition to everything else. Sam, her husband, was ill and not working. Most of their savings were used for Seth's medical bills. She was in the process of putting Seth's house up for sale (the house was in her name). She would soon have to apply for medical assistance for Seth.

Thoughts of retribution kept clouding her mind. She even failed the next county exam she took. Once her friend in management retired, the total stranger who was appointed as the new director proved to be tough, but fair and could not be buttered up under any circumstances. Yetta was forced to actually work. She pronounced the new director 'incompetent' because, unfortunately for Yetta he liked Sheba's work and the way she handled staff.

Yetta became more and more distraught as the days went by. One day she was on top, the next she was slowly sliding toward the bottom. She had to find something to keep her from losing her mind.

****

It was the lunch hour, big busty Rachel's favorite time of day.

"You know she must be giving somebody some kitty. They don't give no jobs to nobody in showbusiness unless you do."

She was addressing a group of women in County Bureau's fifth floor lounge, where they always gathered to eat and gossip, especially gossip. Besides being the carriers of vicious gossip, that same group of women were the *subject* of most of the *worst* gossip.

They sat around and talked about everybody, including each other.What they didn't know for fact, they made up to make the stories juicier. The loud and raucous laughter that resounded from the fifth floor lounge let everybody in the building know that some poor individual was being torn apart.

"Yeah," Rachel continued, "she walks around here like she's better than everybody else. She makes believe she don't go to bed with any men. If she don't, she must be going to bed with women. She got to be at least 35 years old. Who ever heard of a Black woman over fifteen that didn't need a man?"

Everybody started laughing.

While she waited for the laughter to die down, Rachel scooped up some of the potato salad and collard greens from the plastic bowl in front of her and shoved the spoon in her mouth. With her jaws still chewing ferociously, she continued to talk to her audience with a mouth full of food.

They listened, some believed her and some were very skeptical. This was Rachel talking and her mouth was not Bible. She was the epitome of carnal experience. She had been to bed with practically every man in County Bureau #105. Still that didn't mean she knew everything. She had been caught in many a lie. The men that wouldn't have her had also been on the bad end of Rachel's gossip.

She kept her hair dyed red, suprisingly, it went rather well with her brown skin. Her dresses were always low cut to show off half her bust and so short that she did not have to bend down to show her wares on either end. Rachel's bust was tremendous for such a short woman, her rear end was also huge. Her six children did not stop her from getting around, but sometimes her big mouth did.

Although she called herself outspoken and frank, everybody else, including her friends, called her vulgar, loud and vicious.

Her favorite story that she told about herself was that, one night, she was staggering drunk coming home from a bar. She had to walk through a dark alley to get to her door. She was never frightened, drunk or sober. After all, she figured, what did she have to lose?

This time, at 4 A.M., as Rachel reached out for her door, an arm grabbed her from the shadows. The man gruffly pulled her to him and started to fumble with her clothes.

"Mister," Rachel said drunkenly, "If you want to screw me, you are going to have to come inside to my warm bed. I ain't doing nothing out here on this cold sidewalk."

The man, stunned, stood for moment hesitating, then ran. He didn't know what she was up to and wasn't taking any chances.

Rachel shrugged her shoulders and stumbled inside to her bed alone.

When Rachel finished her story about herself, the women laughed.

"Yeah. Like I said, Sheba must be giving somebody some kitty. She gets quite a few little jobs in different movies. I know that Black model on the front cover of Ebony magazine this month. She screwed anybody and everybody, even before she started modeling. That's why she is making so much money now."

"But Rachel, you said yourself, she was like that before. Maybe Sheba isn't like that. She seems to be a very decent woman." This was Stella talking. She still had her husband with her and he was a very good husband, even if he was stingy. At least her own paycheck was her very own to do as she wanted. Every penny she made went into clothes for herself and her small son.

"Decent shit! That's a good act! That woman is on stage every minute." Barbara joined in the conversation. She too, was quite heavy and wore all her clothes two sizes too small. End result, no secrets, but at least her underwear was clean.

"Oh, I don't think anybody could keep up an act twenty-four hours a day, three hundred and sixty-five days a year. She'd go insane." Stella answered.

"You don't think that dizzy dame is crazy?" Barbara asked.

"No, I don't. She is very intelligent and good-natured.Every exam she takes, she not only passes, but she gets the highest ratings around here. Just because she's Black, they give her a hard time. They treat Yetta and Josephine better because they're White."

Stella was very annoyed. She liked to gossip too, but sometimes they went too far. They had no basis for the lies they were telling now. Sheba was a hardworking Black woman, nobody gave her anything. Her promotions were given her only when she passed the exams. She would not do any of the things that Rachel, Barbara, Pearl and Evelyn were claiming she did. They were all extremely jealous of her for many reasons, but especially since she had the respect and admiration of most of the men at County Bureau #105. She started working for the city as an entry clerk, the very bottom of the barrel, moving up through the exams.

"Some people are like that. They can pass those tests and do the work, but that doesn't mean they ain't crazy."

Barbara knew she sounded unreal and stubborn, and that no one believed what she was saying. She was one of the jealous women who felt Sheba was going places and would leave them behind, stuck forever in their current jobs.

But she continued talking anyway. "Besides, Evelyn said she's a real mean bitch and a slave driver."

Ilene Levinson, one of Sheba's White workers answered Barbara. "Evelyn lied. I know because the rest of us in Sheba's unit had to do Evelyn's work for her. She was hardly ever there. I heard they gave Evelyn the job supervising the file room because that's the only place she *has* to work."

Ilene also knew that the spiteful talk she was hearing wasn't just the usual anti-management venting. Sheba somehow had set herself apart with a natural style and intelligence, easily resented by the non-ambitious.

When Sheba first came to County Bureau #105 and her co-workers found out she was interested in the Performing Arts, they laughed at her. Then when she started getting bit and extra parts in movies and television, they began to get jealous.

Worse than Sheba's creative accomplishments was the hold she had over some of the men.

Before Paul left County Bureau, Pearl asked him to do something for her on his lunch hour. He refused.

"You did it for Sheba, why can't you do it for me? What's she giving you that I'm not?" she asked nastily.

Paul's face flashed anger for a split second. Then he said, "A beautiful smile from a beautiful lady. And, for your information, she didn't have to ask me to do anything for her. I volunteered my services."

Pearl turned beet red, and said, "Like shit." Then she walked away from him.

"Hey Pearl, what's the matter with you? You look madder than a wet hen." Marcella shouted this from across the office.

"Don't be so nosey, Marcella."

Marcella shrugged her shoulders and continued talking to her boyfriend, Richard Zimblinsky. She received welfare benefits before she started working at County Bureau #105. Her two kids and she needed more than the welfare checks afforded them. Marcella went to the employment division to ask for help in getting a decent job.

The social workers there arranged for her to take an exam. She passed it and got a job with the county as a clerk.

They began eating better and Marcella bought some new furniture and nice clothes. Her kids didn't have to wear rags any more.

Marcella also had an outside, live-in boyfriend, Bill. Until recently though, he lived with his wife and children. She wasn't satisfied seeing him on weekends only. Not only that, she didn't feel his wife was treating him right, and she told him so, again and again. Bill finally gave in and moved in with Marcella and her kids.

When Bill's wife's mother died, Marcella didn't want Bill to attend the services. She was afraid he might want to stay there.

"Bill, I'm laying down the law. I don't want you to go see that bitch."

"She ain't no bitch, she's my wife. Her mother died, that's my children's grandmother, they're crazy about her. I got to be there." His voice was firm and hard.

"Like Hell. You keep your ass here with me."

Bill looked hard at Marcella. He was thinking about hitting her, but he turned and went out the door.

That was Friday night.

Marcella made the kids go to bed and sat in the livingroom feeling depressed. She gathered all the joints she could find, and a bottle of wine, and drank and smoked everything in front of her.

The next thing Marcella knew, she was in the County Hospital mental ward. They told her she'd been wandering around the streets naked again.

The doctors released her Saturday, she had to get home to her kids. When she arrived home, Bill still hadn't returned. The clothes she was wearing depressed her even more. They couldn't let her go back home naked, so she'd been issued unclaimed clothes from dead people.

Marcella was on the verge of doing some serious harm to herself when the kids stopped her. The sobs and tears of the children made her pull herself together. They needed their mother.

She certainly had her share of troubles. The previous week, the bank repossessed her new car. They embarrased her on the job by towing it out of the parking lot right in front of the County Bureau building.

Bill had begged her not to get that car. He had to pay child support to his wife in addition to helping Marcella with her bills. His small salary could only go so far.

After Bill spent a couple of nights at his wife's house, Marcella began to adopt an "I don't care any more" attitude toward Bill.

One of the White men on the job took an interest in her. He was supervisor of the custodial staff, Richard Zimblinsky. She spent a lot of time in the custodian's room with him. He was a very pleasant man, quiet and so laid back that no one ever said any thing mean about him. He had a gentle and soothing effect on Marcella and they just couldn't get enough of each other. If Richard hadn't already been married, no doubt he would have married Marcella. But there was no way he was going to give up his family, he loved his kids too much. Marcella accepted this after all, she did have a man at home.

****

Loud screams penetrated the air at County Bureau #105, and broke Sheba's concentration on the case before her. She looked up sharply, seeing Raphael and J.C. running toward the stairwell. Most of the staff, including Sheba, followed, not fully out of curiosity, but to see if a worker needed help. Sometimes an irate client would attack a worker.

Ilene Levinson was already on the scene, and said to Sheba, "They're both clients."

The man was banging the woman's head against the cement floor when Raphael and J.C. pulled him off her. They handcuffed him and took him to the patrol room, with the woman sobbing loudly in the background.

Sheba found out that the man had gone out to buy cigarettes after getting money from the woman to buy them. While he was gone, his girlfriend went into the Patrol room. One of his friends, another client, saw her go in, but his name was called and he did not see her when she came out. A few minutes later, when he came back, the patrol room door was closed. His friend came back from the store.

"Man, those guys got your woman in there with the door closed. I heard they take women in there and screw them on the cot."

The man didn't say anything, but waited outside the door for a long time. He left and went into the toilet and when he came out, the patrol room door was open. That's when he spotted his girlfriend going to the stairwell. He ran up behind her, grabbed her by the hair, and started beating her unmercifully.

As it turned out, she was in the bathroom while the patrol room door was closed. She had only stopped by the patrol room for a few seconds to inquire where the bathroom was located.

Downstairs, in the ABD units, after the air cleared, and the Jewish holidays were over, Sheba and Josephine managed to maintain a civil, professional relationship. Josephine behaved as if she hadn't done anything wrong, still expecting Sheba to drive her home every night. Of course, Sheba did drive her home every night. She didn't want her conscience whipping her if anything happened to Josephine.

A new office manager came in and Sheba had at least one ally at County Bureau #105. Mrs. Cohen, a Jew, agreed with Sheba that she had been treated unfairly during the Jewish holidays and took all written documentation out of Sheba's personnel file.

****

Today, as Sheba passed Josephine's desk to get to her own, she noticed that Josephine looked upset over something. Sheba kept on walking because Josephine was always upset over something. She let everybody and everything irritate her, and Sheba was tired of being the recipient of all Josephine's woeful tales.

Josephine came from hardy, Irish stock, with a very strict father. He did everything within his power to protect his daughter's virginity until the day she was married. On the other hand, his sons were encouraged to assert their manhood.

At the age of 18, Josephine completed high school and obtained a job in a factory's office as assistant to the bookkeeper. She didn't mind the job, but she did mind the fact that her father took her whole paycheck and handed her back a dollar for lunch and car fare. In those days, 1928, you could get a hot dog or hamburger for a nickel. Her father would tell her to wash it down with some water.

Whenever she needed clothing, she had to beg him for money. He always had to know why she couldn't make do with what she already owned. The older girls she worked with wore pretty dresses, while Josephine was stuck with all her older sister's hand-me-downs.

She began to hate her father with a passion. He had his own plumbing business and made plenty of money, even during the late twenties and thirties.

When her father died, a few years later, she controlled her own paycheck and learned how to save. She went to night school and studied dressmaking in order to take full advantage of her mother's sewing machine. Her bank account grew fast.

As shrewd as Josephine was with her income, she allowed one of her co-workers to dupe her out of five hundred dollars of her hard-earned money.

She was sitting at her desk, eating lunch in the office, when Laura, a worker from the factory, came into the office. They often had lunch together when Laura wasn't going to lunch with one of the men who worked in the factory with her.

"Josephine, I want to ask you a favor."

"What is it?" Josephine was on guard. She could guess what was coming knowing that her constant bragging about her bank account must have touched a nerve in Laura. At the time, it gave Josephine great pleasure to tell her friend about her financial achievements.

"Look, Josephine, my brother wants to borrow some money from me, but I know he won't pay me back."

"So? What has that got to do with me?" Josephine went on munching her sandwich.

"Would you lend it to him? He'll pay you back."

Josephine stopped munching and looked at Laura with raised eyebrows, "You think I'm a fool? If he won't pay you back, I know he won't pay me back either!"

Laura began pleading.

"He'd pay you back, Josephine. You're not related to him. I'm his sister, he thinks I owe him a living for some strange reason.

"How much does he want to borrow?" Josephine sipped her tea.

"Five hundred dollars."

"What?" Food and tea splattered out of Josephine's mouth, some of it hitting Laura.

Josephine hurriedly reached for her handkerchief and wiped her mouth. She stared at Laura incredulously.

Laura began to feel a little uneasy. She got up from the chair saying, "You think about it, I'll see you at five o'clock."

Josephine stared at Laura until she went out the door. Five hundred dollars! Was she crazy?

It took her a long time to save up that money. Let her brother find some other way to get the money.

Unfortunately, Laura was persistent. She said her brother kept nagging her and she kept nagging Josephine, who dreaded each time Laura came into her office.

"Tell him to go to a bank." Josephine said annoyed. "They'll lend him the money."

"He tried, but they turned him down."

"Then you lend it to him and tell him that it came from me."

"He would know and I won't get it back."

"I'll hold your bank book for you."

Laura worked on Josephine until she broke her down.

Josephine gave into Laura to get her off her back. After she lent Laura's brother the money, Laura dodged her.

She called Laura's house, but someone else always answered the telephone.

When she finally managed to corner Laura on the job, Laura's attitude was very nasty.

"Look Laura, when are you going to pay me my money?"

"Pay you? I don't owe you any money."

"Yes you do! Five hundred dollars!"

"I didn't borrow that. You lent that to my brother!"

"Yes, but you asked for it." Josephine was angry.

61

Laura walked away from Josephine saying, "Well, I don't know when he'll pay you. He left town."

"What?"

Josephine went to a lawyer, but nothing could be done except to chalk it up as a bad debt.

Never again did Josephine loan anyone anything. She was so tight with her money after that, she managed to save quite a bit and even invested in some stock.

When she was 28 years old, she went on a cruise to the Bahamas and met her husband. He was an architect making a very comfortable salary. Together they had four children, two boys and two girls. The three older children had completed college when her husband died. Both boys were married. Josephine was 60 years old and had to find a way to support herself and her youngest daughter, who was now 16.

Josephine took her husband's death badly. Catherine, her youngest daughter, felt the negative effects of her mother's constant whining and inability to make decisions.

Sadly her mother didn't know what to counsel when Catherine started dating boys, so the child took it upon herself to make her own decisions. Josephine had moved to a low income neighborhood, the boys there were rougher and tougher. Catherine's decisions were not always in her best interest.

It was about that time that drugs, were penetrating deprived areas. Catherine's boyfriends introduced her first to pot then to heroin.

Josephine tried to talk to her but Catherine would start using obscenities and shout her mother down every time.

At one point, Josephine threw Catherine out of the house. Catherine had started beating up her mother for money. Josephine called her sons and they physically threw Catherine out. She took Catherine back in when the girl said she was pregnant and had no one else to turn to for help.

The dividends from the stocks and bonds were not enough to support them and a new baby, so Josephine applied for and received a job at County Bureau #105.

When Josephine found out that Catherine had lied to her about being pregnant, she was both angry and relieved at the same time. She demanded that her daughter return to school to complete her education and determined to stop giving Catherine spending money. For that, Catherine beat her up again.

Josephine went to work with a black eye the next day. As she sat working at her desk, she looked up and saw Catherine standing there, watching her.

"What are you doing here?" She asked her daughter gingerly.

"I want some money, now, bitch!" Catherine glowered menacingly at Josephine.

"I don't have any money to give you." Josephine felt very uneasy, she did not want Catherine to make another scene here.

"Bitch! I said I want some money and I want it NOW!" Catherine's stringy blond hair fell in her eyes as she moved threateningly.

"Catherine, go home. I'll talk to you there." Josephine was highly nervous now and so was the rest of the staff. This would not be the first time Catherine had made an appearance at County Bureau #105.

Behind Catherine, Ronald, Josephine's co-worker, had watched her as she walked toward Josephine. He was already out of his chair.

When Catherine slapped her mother, Ronald grabbed her and pulled her away. By then, the patrolmen were there and ready to call the police.

"Please don't do that." Josephine begged. "She didn't mean it, she'll go home." Turning to Catherine, she pleaded, "You will go home like a good girl, won't you?"

Catherine looked at her with such disdain that Josephine could have died on the spot.

The patrolmen marched Catherine to the door and said that if she ever came back, they would call the precinct and have her locked up in jail for disturbing the peace. They didn't have to worry about her. She got money somewhere else to buy the drugs she wanted, then took an overdose of heroin.

Catherine's body was found behind some garbage cans not far from where Josephine lived. Her death nearly killed Josephine. She completely forgot all the bad things her daughter said and did to her, and told everybody Catherine had been a good daughter.

Nobody reminded her of how her daughter had really behaved, so she was able to endure the after math of grief with denial.

Josephine visited her eldest daughter's home occasionally on weekends, her daughter asked her to stay with them. Betty was married with two small children. It was a very happy marriage, when a horrible situation began.

Josephine's daughter, Betty, was quite a beautiful woman, petite and very shapley. Her husband, Steve, rugged and handsome, was very much in love with her and gave her everything her heart desired.

When the youngest child entered school, Steve and Betty decided they wanted to start going out together again. Just the two of them.

Betty happened to mention this to one of the children's teachers who was a novice at the parochial school.

"Mrs. Gallagher, I would be more than happy to watch the children for you on weekends."

"Would you be able to do that? Don't you live at the convent?" Betty asked.

"Yes, I do, but we are allowed to go outside of the convent."

"Oh, Sister, that would be wonderful to have someone I can trust taking care of the children."

The nun babysat whenever Betty and Steve went out. Josephine began to spend weekends with her brother and his family out in the country. The Sister would sometimes drop in to see Betty and the children even when they didn't go out. Steve always drove her back to the convent.

Betty and the nun got along so well that Betty would lend the Sister her clothes, both wearing a size four.

Six months later, Steve upset everybody when he dropped a bombshell.

He requested a divorce from Betty so that he could marry the nun!

Shocked, Betty could not believe her ears.

"You must be crazy! Why the Sister would be shocked to hear you talk like this." Betty gasped.

"She told me to ask you."

"What! I dont believe you."

"Yes. You must be going with some other woman and trying to be funny. Well, you are not funny. This is a terribly evil thing for you to say and do."

"Why? She is only human and a very lovely woman. We couldn't help ourselves."

"She is a nun. Couldn't either of you respect that? She is supposed to be married to God." Betty burst into tears, ran into the bedroom and locked the door. Her heart was pounding furiously from the shock and horror of the situation.

The door remained locked and Steve made no further attempts to talk to her again that night.

In the morning, she waited until she was sure he had left for work before she opened the door.

When Betty broke the news to Josephine, they were both extremely upset. Their religion did not permit divorce, and here was a woman of the church breaking up a marriage and trying to force Betty into filing.

Betty called the convent and spoke to the Mother Superior of the convent, who in turn spoke to the Priest. They spoke to the nun and threatened to excommunicate her and Steve if they did not break up the affair.

The nun refused to give Steve up.

Betty refused to divorce Steve.

Steve left Betty, but was hit with large child support and alimony payments.The nun was exiled from the church, forced to get a job to help Steve with the bills. They were miserable together.

****

1979

Sheba begins work at BCS

Back at County Bureau #105, Marcella was assigned to work with Sheba. Marcella didn't mind. She liked her, even though she knew a few of the women were jealous of Sheba. Marcella had no problems with her. Richard liked Marcella, Marcella liked Richard. Sheba only spoke to Richard on a professional basis, unlike some of the others, trying to turn his head around.

As long as Marcella did her work, she got along fine with Sheba.

Sometimes they had long conversations when work was slow. They would discuss the goals they wanted to reach and how they wanted to accomplish them. Marcella said she wanted to buy a house on long island and was saving every dime to that end.

Sheba's goals were more complex because she had several different creative talents to work with in acting, singing, writing plays and stories, and composing songs. The arts are highly competitive fields and although Sheba managed to get some work, she still could not afford to leave her job. She had her daughter to support by herself, having divorced her husband when Donna was 2.

Marcella related to her because she had children of her own to support. Bill said he was getting a divorce from his wife, maybe he and Marcella would get married soon. If so, she would stop going with her office boyfriend, Richard.

Everything was going fine at home until Marcella found another woman's shoes in their car. She confronted Bill.

"Whose shoes are these?" she demanded, holding them in front of his face.

Bill was stretched out on the sofa reading the Sunday newspaper.

"Aren't they yours?" he asked innocently.

"You know damn well my feet can't get into these shoes."

"So?"

"So I found these in the car. Who are you running around with?"

"You."

"Don't try to be funny. Where was your ass last night?"

"I told you. I was out with Jerry and the boys."

"No you weren't. He called here last night asking for you."

Bill shook his head disgustedly. He thought he'd told Jerry to cover for him. That lame brain probably forgot.

Marcella didn't let up on Bill. She nagged him constantly, until Bill took to consuming vast amount of hard liquor. He even stopped paying the rent and other bills until Marcella threatened to throw him out in the street, then he gave her money for rent only. She took that as grudgingly as he gave it, but refused to have sex with him, and he stayed out more than ever.

At the office, Marcella became friendly with Lynelle, who happened to be homosexual. Lynelle always wore expensive clothing that was severely tailored. Her voice was as heavy and crisp as a man's, and her features were extremely hard.

Lynelle claimed that she was extremely wealthy and did not need her job as a bottomline clerk at County Bureau #105. Besides this job, she worked full time at night for a bank where her salary was almost three times what she made at County Bureau #105. In addition, she said she had been married once, she claimed her husband had died and left her a fortune.

Gossip had it that Lynelle had purchased a home in another state for a woman who was her lover. Thus she had two households to support and surely needed both jobs to manage.

Since Marcella had now become hard up for cash, she was vunerable to Lynelle's advances to her. They became fast friends.

She needed a lump sum of money to pay off her debts. Bill wasn't coming through for her and Marcella was turned down at the banks and credit union. Lynelle said she would give her as much money as she needed, but Marcella would have to do as she asked. Marcella agreed, because she was desperate for the money, and she was curious as to what lesbians did in bed.

After Marcella formed her alliance with Lynelle, her mind weakened further and she began to lose control.

She talked to herself constantly and made all the workers within earshot uneasy. Her appointments at the out-patient mental clinic were either forgotten or ignored. She was slowly slipping into oblivion, her marijana use helping to deteriorate her mental condition.

Sheba was very much aware of Marcella's condition and cared about what was happening to her. She tried to engage her in a conversation like they used to have on occasion, but Marcella wasn't interested. There was nothing else Sheba could do for her without endangering herself. Lynelle carried a handgun strapped to her ankle.

The clique that Marcella involved herself with consisted, allegedly, of bi-sexual women. Marcella, like most of the women in the group, had been heterosexual, most had children. She would sit at her desk, and when one of the clique passed by, such as Rachel, she would hoot and holler at her backside, just like a man.

"Um-um. Look at that. Boy oh boy!" Marcella would yell.

Rachel would smile back at Marcella and twist her rear end even more, rolling her eyes simultaneously.

"Yeah, yeah, yeah, baby," Rachel answered.

Sheba went on doing her work, and as long as Marcella did her work, they got along.

Problems arose when Marcella's social life began taking precedence over her work while she was on duty at County Bureau #105. Sheba didn't know whether or not Marcella was on prescribed tranquilizers or or illegal drugs, but at times Marcella seemed to be on a different planet.

One day, Sheba had an urgent request at four o'clock for some papers. She instructed Marcella to pull them from the file immediately. Marcella sat in her chair chewing and smacking loudly on a piece of fruit and didn't budge. In fact, upon finishing the fruit, she proceeded to make two phone calls. Disgusted, Sheba gave the task to another worker. "I'm gonna' do it," Marcella protested through her fog.

This was the last straw, Sheba thought. She would have to speak to her latest supervisor, Edith Black.

Edith was a short, plump, Black woman who never, ever consorted with Black men. All of her male lovers were White. Except the man she married. She thought of herself as bi-sexual since she went with men and women.

She worked her way up from a secretarial position to provisional Associate Office Manager. Her tremendous consumption of alcohol was well-known at the Main County Office in the city, this prevented her from moving up to better positions.

Her desk drawers held a large supply of scotch, bourbon and other liquors. She would frequently drink whiskey to the point of blacking out right at her desk in County Bureau #105. Edith would say that this was from high blood pressure, but Marcella had told Sheba that Edith blacked out only when she drank large amounts of alcohol.

Each time this happened, she would be taken to the local hospital, giving her an excuse to take anywhere from two to four weeks off work.

Edith was at every office party, consuming vast amounts of liquor. The supply of whisky she kept in her desk did not satisfy her so she would disappear each afternoon. Along with her cronies and after a long lunch hour, she'd go into the stockroom and lock the door.

The stockroom's wall was plastered with pictures of nude women in every conceivable pose (some were inconceivable). The woman were all colors and ages, ranging in size from very fat to very skinny.

During Edith's visits, supplies were impossible to obtain since the door was locked from inside. Associate Office Manager or not, she did more to impede progress at County Bureau #105 than anyone else.

One of her drinking buddies (and she favored all of them with special jobs), was a Black woman, Helen.

Helen was straight, but Edith liked to talk to her. She knew Helen would not discuss her personal affairs, she'd damn well not.

No one at County Bureau #105 knew Edith's backround, except Helen and Edith's male Jewish lover, Sidney Dwyer.

When Edith was 16, she had a baby out of wedlock by her steady boyfriend at the time, Stanley. He refused to marry her and even denied that he was the father of her son, who was diagnosed with Mongoloidism. Stanley wanted to be a doctor and felt that he did not want to be burdened with a wife and baby.

Edith was heartbroken, both over the baby's condition and being rejected completely by Stanley.

Edith's family was upper middle class, although they did not condone having babies out of wedlock, her parents tried to be understanding, and made the very best they could out of a tough situation.

They convinced her to continue her education, so she finished high school and completed a secretarial course. She started working for the County when she was 19 years old. Her son was then almost 3 years old.

Another tragedy struck when her parents were both killed in an automobile accident.

This was when Edith first took to the bottle. It was practically impossible for her to find a suitable babysitter for Stanley Jr. She was forced to take an eight-month leave-of absence.

Finally, she found a kindly, elderly lady to take care of her son and she went back to work. She had inherited the private house from her parents, a life insurance policy and a large sum of money from the car accident.

Now years later, her son was 28 years old and unable to do much for himself, except stay home and play with his toys. She had tried putting him in a institution for awhile, but on visiting days, he always begged to come home. He said that the staff was cruel to him, and she inquired about the bruise, and was told he fell down, she brought him home.

His coordination was bad, but not that bad.

She managed to find someone to stay with him during the day while she was at work.

Whenever she felt that her situation was overwhelming her, she would board Junior out and take off for the Caribbean islands. If she couldn't afford that, she took it out on the staff at the office, which was pretty often.

Evelyn was one of Edith's drinking buddies and had psyched Edith against Sheba for personal reasons.

Since Evelyn was transferred out of Sheba's unit, she was forced to work.

In Edith's alcoholic mind, she felt that Sheba would eventually take her job away from her. The idea that Sheba didn't drink also bothered her. She joined the growing number of people at County Bureau #105 that called Sheba 'Miss Sactimonious' because she did not indulge in any of the clique's favorite pastimes.

Fortunately for Sheba, she did not permit anyone to pry into her personal affairs, so no one knew whether or not she had any vices. Try as she did, Edith could not get any legitimate dirt on Sheba.

The rumors about Sheba and Paul or the stud Rafael, did not amount to anything in Edith's opinion. Sheba was far too intelligent to let herself get involved with a man who had no respect for anybody, including himself.

Edith's own lover at the office, Sidney, was a mild-tempered milquetoast, subservient to her in job title. She needed him to make her feel important. They would kiss openly, in front of the staff, without shame.

Sometimes Edith's behavior was schizophrenic. One moment, she would be sitting behind her desk in full control and behaving in a cold manner. The next, she would be leaning back in her chair, dress at the top of her thighs, laughing bawdily, unable to make any intelligent decisions.

When she was in the latter mood, her drinking buddies would flock to her, knowing she had bottles handy. This was also when they could get her to do whatever they wanted.

If there was someone they wanted her to put the screws to, she would do it at that moment with pleasure.

As a result she got bounced back to Assistant Office Manager for leaning too hard on the wrong person at the wrong time.

Her replacement was Mrs.Cohen, very cool, intelligent woman with foresight as well as hindsight.

In the meantime, County Bureau #105 had no Director for a long time. The former director had died the year before and the incumbent Offfice Manager also had to act as Director, wearing "two hats".

When County Bureau #105's staff heard they were getting Robert Dunn for their new Director, they had mixed emotions. He was a goodlooking, divorced Black man, but straight from the main office. Most of the staff knew him by reputation and name. The reports about his personality were positive, but the fact that he had worked in the main office made him suspect to some people.

The conscientious staff did not have to worry. Robert Dunn set out to reassure them that as long as they were cooperative, did their work and made him look good to the Main Office, he would be fair and fully cooperate with the staff.

His tall, lean frame was a pleasure to look at anytime. He was ruggedly handsome, not just a pretty boy, with piercing grey eyes which stood out against the surrounding brown skin. His hair was worn natural in a short cropped cut, with a few grey hairs for distinction.

Shortly before Robert Dunn arrived at County Bureau #105, Sheba was promoted to Associate Office

Manager after passing the exam. Mrs.Cohen, the Office Manager, did not want to demote any of the current Associates, although one of them had failed the exam. She asked Sheba if she would take the newly open position of Training Specialist and Consultant.

Sheba was delighted to accept. It meant that she no longer had to supervise staff, write up performance evaluations, disciplinary reports, etc., had her own private office.

At first she was totally on her own, with a wide latitude to create lesson plans, schedule training sessions and perform elbow training with personal consultations for the entire staff.

After Mr.Dunn's arrival, Sheba found that she was under his direct supervision. He called her into his office almost immediately after he arrived.

"Mrs. Welters, I'm glad you were chosen for the job. Mrs.Cohen recommended you highly and it makes me deeply happy that you accepted."

Sheba looked directly into his wonderful grey eyes that seemed to look deep down into her very soul. It was a struggle to maintain her cool. She just couldn't seem to wipe the smile off her face. He seemed to be aware of how she felt because he was continuing to smile at her.

"Thank you Mr. Dunn." She wondered if this man was as warm and sincere as he was coming across to her at the moment. She sensed that he needed her support, she knew how hostile Edith and her friends could be! Sheba decided she would give the man a chance. Maybe he was for real, that would be a welcome change.

"Please don't call me Mr.Dunn, call me Bob."

Sheba wanted to like Bob. She was tired of having to be on guard constantly, afraid that her words would be twisted to someone else's advantage and used to work against her for no good reason. This frequently happened when the clique was in the supply room on one of their infamous drinking bouts. In that mood, they were ready to crucify everybody.

Sheba had stopped eating in the lounge a long time ago and now ate alone. Some of the women used filthy obscenities referring to men, and because they knew Sheba disliked to hear that sort of thing, they used it non-stop. Sheba was called "too sensitive", and was told she must have a hangup. It was an awful experience to sit and listen to them disclosing their private and most intimate affairs to the world at large. Later, the others would discuss the details with anybody who hadn't heard it personally. The facts would be twisted and situations changed to make the story more interesting.

Sheba hadn't bothered to enter their conversations, not even to clarify facts she knew were being deliberately twisted. They would certainly repeat it, then pretend she initiated the gossip. She showed a certain reserve and it made them steer clear of her, even though curiosity burned them up. Her private life was her own business, including her daughter Donna. The women were constantly inquiring about her sex life, or rather if she had one, straight or otherwise.

The women in the lounge couldn't understand where Sheba was coming from. Even when Sheba had sat down and explained her views about life, her values and the fact that she wanted someone who would share those with her, the ladies of the lounge would not have understood or believed anything she told them. It was clear to her that those very values were fast becoming unique.

Her thoughts went back to the day before, Ilene and Barbara had come to her office to ask a question.

One of the client's children had stolen $1,200 from his grandmother.The child was caught with what was left of the money. He had purchased a $200 stereo among other things.

His grandmother had recieved a lump sum of twelve hundred dollars from the Social Security Office. It was retroactive payment for old age benefits. She had cashed the check and put the money in a dresser drawer, her grandson 12 years old, saw the money and took every dollar.

Sheba said to Ilene, "Well, the merchant who sold him a $200 stereo should be punished. Where did he think a 12 year old boy would get $200 in cash?

Barbara looked at Sheba as if she thought Sheba was insane.

"Why shouldn't he sell his stuff? That's why he's in business to make money."

"He should know better than to deal with a child that age when that kind of money is involved. It is more than likely to be stolen money and the police will confiscate that money along with the merchandise." Sheba answered.

"Nobody's perfect. Not even you." Barbara answered.

"Yeah, everybody and I do mean everybody's got some kind of vice. If you don't do one thing, you do another. Drugs, alcohol, you take your pick". Ilene chimed in to agree with Barbara. Ilene was the only white woman in the clique.

Ilene was remembering how Rafael used to talk to her about Sheba and how he was dying to lay her. It made her furious, especially since she, Ilene, was in bed with him at the time.

She could hear him saying, determinedly, as he moved his huge hands over her body. "I'm still gonna try to get Sheba. I won't be satisfied till I lay her."

"Leave that Black bitch alone, you got me." Ilene reprimanded him.

"That means I got exactly nothin'." Rafael laughed.

"You M...F..." She reached up to slap his face, and he grabbed her wrists. He further humiliated her by throwing her out of bed, *her* bed.

In spite of this, Ilene would not believe a word Rafael said. Sheba was Black and she was White. He was just saying those things to make her jealous. Besides, she had always been told she was very beautiful, her pale skin, covered with several layers of makeup, assured her of this daily when she looked into her mirror.

She needed the constant reassurance, her night-time job demanded that she looked good. She had taken over where Shirley left off. Prostitution paid well.

Ilene loved Robert Dunn's good looks. If she only knew, he wasn't interested in her, except as a worker. His mind, too, was on Sheba. From the first moment he saw her, he was attracted to Sheba Welters. She seemed to be conservative and reserved. He wondered if he would be able to break through that reserve. That first day he'd met her, he had gone home thinking about her.

Robert Dunn had been married once, his ex-wife had been impossible for him to live with. When he found out that she had had an abortion without consulting him, he decided he had had enough. He was now back home with his parents, who were self-supporting. They owned the big roomy house that he was born in, 43 years ago.

Since the breakup of his marriage, he'd dated many women. Some he had considered for a longer term relationship but not really being in love with them, rejected the thought.

His outward attitude toward Sheba was professional. He didn't want to crowd her or scare her, she impressed him as being a little shy. Today, he complimented her and she blushed so furiously that the blood showed through her brown skin. But she smiled and said, "Thank you," anyway. He couldn't know it was because she felt attracted to him, that she had blushed.

He was going to go slow, very slow. After all was said and done, he would not want her to think that he did not have honorable intentions. This strong feeling he had for her was new to him. He didn't feel this way even when he married his ex-wife.

Evaluation for work performance came when Bob Dunn had only been on the job at County Bureau for two months. He was responsible for Sheba's evaluation in her new position. Her work really was outstanding, he felt he couldn't say enough good things about her. When Bob Dunn's secretary brought the papers to her, she could not believe her eyes. It was the best evaluation Sheba had, ever heard of anyone getting on the County payroll. In addition, he had added a memo to elucidate and justify 18, outstanding points on the standard 'Performance Report' form.

Sheba took in a deep breath of air and continued reading. The memo went on to say, after two pages of detailed and eloquently written praise and recommendations:

Mrs. Welters has displayed a great deal of maturity, responsibility, talent and knowledge in the performance of her duties. She is definitely high above average in her supervisory and management abilities and is well-respected by both her superiors and subordinates.

In addition, Mrs. Welters has enlisted the interest and cooperation of other supervisory staff in the center to help conduct training sessions with her.

County Bureau #105 has had people from Resource, Employment, Housing, Control Unit and the Director's office also speak to the classes on material pertinent to their own fields of operations.

In view of the foregoing, therefore, we recommend that Mrs. Sheba Welters be given an above-standard evaluation, and promotion to Assistant Director, with private office.

Robert M. Dunn
Director, County Bureau
#105

Bob knew that every word of it was true. Sheba was a fantastic worker, even taking work home with her when necessary. At least now she would know that her effort was appreciated. As for his personal feelings, he guessed that that side of it would take a bit more doing. He had broken down her outer reserve and he felt that she trusted him, but he wasn't sure how much.

If he approached her too soon for a date, he might ruin his chances with her entirely. Bob wasn't certain, at this stage, how far he would be willing to go himself. One thing was sure, each night he had to go home, he didn't want to leave her.

The few days Sheba didn't work at that office were miserable for him.

As for Sheba, as she read her work evaluation, joy began to bubble up inside her until it reached her mouth and she couldn't help smiling with great happiness. She walked over Bob, on impulse, and kissed him on his cheek, and he touched her hand lightly.

"Thank you, Bob. Really. I have never seen anything like it before."

"Are you satisfied? Do you think I should add anything?" He was sincere.

"Add anything? This is enough to make me President of the United States of America, with an office to call my own!"

They laughed together.

He wondered if he should ask her out now. No, he guessed that she might feel obligated to go, even if she really didn't want to.

They chatted for a while, then she left to go back to her desk. He felt elated, maybe he was getting somewhere. Maybe he was being presumptuous, just because of a little kiss on the cheek, but after knowing her for a few months, he'd made more progress with her than any other man at this location.

Back in her office, Sheba was tingling, too. She'd just lost all her cool and truthfully, she was enjoying the warm feelings surging through her. She did not want to believe what was happening to her.

Every time she entered Bob's office, he would lift his head up from his work, and the penetrating gaze from his magnificent grey eyes shot through her like an electricity shock. How in the world could she keep her cool when he looked at her like that?

In all the years since her divorce, she had dated only one man. That unfortunately, had turned out to be a wrestling match on the first and last date. She did not consider the invitation to Paul's mother's bar-b-que a real date.

She'd decided to be a lot more careful in the future.

She had a lot of thinking to do, because as sure as Christmas was coming, so was Bob's request for a date.

Neither Sheba or Bob were aware that just as Sheba bent over to kiss Bob on the cheek, Duke, County Bureau #105 messenger, was passing by the door and saw them.

Duke was married and had kids, but he too, had his share of women at County Bureau #105, as well as a steady girlfriend.

As much as he wanted to, he had never tried to get anywhere with Sheba, but strangely enough, he adored her as though she was an untouchable goddess. Seeing her kiss the Director like that made him rage inside even though it was only on the cheek.

Duke was a sharp dresser and considered himself a very cool, laid back guy. He was responsible for supplying a lot of the staff with an assortment of illegal drugs, and also had an illegal numbers racket going. In addition, he did a little side profiteering with clients. Duke would arrive very early in the morning to give out numbers to the clients. Only a certain amount of clients could be seen each day, therefore when the numbers ran out, the remaining clients would be turned away.

Duke would sell numbers to clients at fifty cents a ticket. He gave out up to one hundred everyday. Duke made more with his numbers and drugs, than he did being a messenger. But he played the game cool and careful and never got caught. He knew he had to keep this job as a cover.

Willie, another messenger, stopped him in the hall.

"Say, man. Let me have some stuff. I'll give you the money payday."

"You know better than that. You don't get any stuff without bread." Duke's voice was quiet, hard and firm. Serious, no joking.

"Come on Duke, you know I'll pay you."

"Yeah, Willie. I heard that shit before. Soon as you get your check, you split for the day. Next time I saw you your bread was all gone."

"I had to pay my rent, man. It ain't gonna' happen again." Willie pleaded.

Duke sucked his teeth and started walking away. Willie reached out for him.

"If you touch me, Nigger, I'll kill you."

Insulted, WIllie started to reach down in his sock and felt cold steel against his temple. Perspiration poured down the sides of his face. Duke knew that Willie kept a ten inch blade in his sock.

"I ought to blow your friggin' head off", said Duke coolly. "But I don't want to lose my job.If you make me get fired, your ass won't be worth shit."

"Duke, I ain't gonna blow your job. Please man, I'm cool… I'm cool."

He let Willie straighten up, then watched him walk away.

That same afternoon, Willie came running back into the county office, sobbing, the tears streaming down his cheeks.

He said two men robbed him and took eighteen hundred dollars in checks, and all the petty cash he had in the satchel he used to deliver office papers.

The office manager seemed to believe him and called the police. After the police left, Willie was told to go home for the day as he didn't seem to be in any condition to work.

On his way out, he stopped by the supply room where Duke had his desk. He threw some dollar bills in front of Duke on the desk.

"Here's your money, man. Give me my stuff."

Duke looked at him and smiled. Willie had stolen the satchel himself. After counting the money, he threw a packet of dope on the table.

"Get the hell out of here before you get me in trouble, too. Nigger."

Willie grabbed the stuff and hurried out.

Shortly after, Rose, Duke's office girlfriend, came in to see him.

"Are you going by the room tonight?"

Although Rose lived with her parents and Duke lived with his wife and kids, he kept a cheap apartment in the neighborhood. This enabled him to spend some free time with Rose, a woman working on a visa from Finland, waiting to get her permanent citizenship papers.

At 50 Duke was twice Rose's age. Rose, tall, slender, shapely and blond, was strangely attracted to him. He liked her because she was just the opposite of what he was in every way. She was White, he was Black, and, she was totally unambitious.

Rose's brownish gold hair hung loose down her back, touching her waistline. She spoke with a slavic accent and had a passion for animals which Duke shared.

Duke would buy dog food to feed the pack of mongrel dogs that roamed the streets around County Bureau #105. (Given that fact, one had to be exceptionally careful where they stepped) On a hot day, the strong smell of dog feces permeated the air.

Duke talked gruffly to Rose in front of other people to show that he was the "Boss". She acted subservient to him just to please him, knowing it was his ego talking. Otherwise, he was very good to her, buying her expensive gifts, including a new car. Her own salary went into the bank every payday.

Although Duke did not use any of the drugs he pushed, he smoked heavily, three and a half packs of cigarettes each day. It was beginning to tell on him. He began to feel so badly that both Rose and his wife were on his back to see a doctor. He finally relented.

The doctor gave Duke a thorough examination, then recommended that he go for X-rays.

"What's wrong, doc?" Duke asked worriedly.

"I'm not sure, but I"ll make an appointment at the hospital for you tomorrow."

"Tomorrow? Can't it wait?"

"I'm afraid not."

"Well, what do you think is wrong with me?"

"I'd rather wait until I see the X-rays."

Duke decided not to press the doctor, he really did not feel like hearing bad news.

He showed up bright and early next day at the hospital for his appointment. His own doctor was there.

It was late in the afternoon when Duke was approached by a nurse. He had been sitting around since they took his X-rays.

"Mr. Browne, would you come with me, please?"

He was nervous, but he followed her anyway. She led him into a small office, just big enough for a tiny desk and three chairs, one behind the desk, He sat on one of the others.

"Mr. Browne, there was something on the X-rays that needs further attention. Dr. Hope would like to admit you to the hospital today."

"Today? I couldn't do that I have to make preparations. My family would be too worried."

"You may call them."

"Why the big rush?"

"It seems urgent."

"What do you mean 'urgent'?"

"The doctor will explain the situation to you." She picked up the phone and dialed three numbers.

"Is Dr. Hope still there?… May I speak to him please? This is Nurse Crowley… Doctor? This is Nurse Crowley. I have Mr. Browne in my office, he doesn't wish to be admitted to the hospital today. I told him you would explain the situation to him… You'll be right down? Thank you, doctor."

She put the phone down gently and turned to Duke.

"He'll be right down."

It seemed like days until the doctor arrived. Duke had an ominous feeling.

Doctor Hope's face was placid and told Duke nothing. He stood up as the physician entered the room.

"Mr. Browne, I didn't mean to worry you, but I would like to have you stay in the hospital for a few days."

"But why? What's wrong?"

"There's a spot on your lungs and I'd like to do a biopsy."

Duke thought this over. For the first time in his life he was really frightened.

"You think there's cancer?"

"I am almost sure of it. How many cigarettes do you smoke a day?"

"Three and a half packs."He didn't see any point in lying about it.

"Three and a half packs a day! Whew! That's an awful lot of tar and nicotine."

"Look, doc, can't I come back another day for the other tests?"

"I would advise you to stay now. The faster you're treated, the better your chances are to improve your condition or at least prevent you from getting any worse."

Duke thought about all the drugs he had in both of his apartments. He wanted to get rid of those first. Besides he had to tell the numbers banker that he was going to be away for awhile.

"Doc, can't you get me admitted another day? I really have to take care of a lot of things before I stay in the hospital."

The doctor sighed.

"It's up to you Mr. Browne. I certainly can't force you to stay and be treated. Whenever you call me, I'll try to get you admitted as soon as possible. We happen to have a couple of empty beds today.

Relieved, Duke said. "Okay. Doc. I'll call you as soon as I wind up a few things."

"Mr. Browne, let me caution you against smoking. Cut it out completely. It is very dangerous for you."

"Thanks, doc. I'll quit."

"I know. One way or another." The doctor was very grim.

Duke almost ran out of the hospital, into the street. He had already forgotten the doctor's warning as he stopped to light a cigarette.

Six months later, Duke still hadn't called the doctor or even visited him, although he felt terrible and was now spitting up blood. He was still smoking, four packs a day now, his physical condition deteriorating rapidly. Dukes weight went from 225 pounds to 130 pounds during those six months since he last saw the doctor. His skin had an ashen hue, everyone at County Bureau #105 pitied him, including WIllie.

Duke started staying home from work most of the time, lying in bed all day. At night, he could not sleep.

Finally, his wife called the doctor against his wishes. She couldn't take it anymore, he was even beginning to wet the bed.

Duke had stopped running numbers and selling dope. Hardly any money was coming into the house, and Mary would have to get a job or the family would have to go on welfare. When she voiced this to Duke, he told her about three safe deposit boxes he had filled with money. On the way to the doctor's office, he had all the boxes signed over to her.

In the doctor's office, Duke could hardly lift his hand to take his shirt off. Doctor Hope called an ambulance as soon as he completed the examination. Duke went into the doctor's bathroom, coughing uncontrollably.

Listening to the racking, heartrending cough, the doctor addressed Duke's wife.

"Why did you wait so long?"

"He begged me not to call. He didn't want to go to the hospital, he's afraid he won't ever come home again."

"I might have been able to help him six months ago."

"Does that mean you can't help him now?"

"It sounds as if his lungs are almost gone.Now we can only try to stop him from suffering so much."

Mary started to cry softly.

As the stretcher rolled Duke to the ambulance, she felt as if he was gone already.

Two weeks later Duke *was* gone.

Rose managed to get her citizenship papers and transferred out to another office. Three months later, she married a man right off the boat from Romania. After all, she needed someone to help pay her bills.

****

Harold Stein was a Social Worker at County Bureau #105. Before the city decided to use clerical staff to interview clients for determining eligbility for receiving financial benefits, preparing budgets and financial grants for eligible clients; and assigning responsibilty for authorizing and issuing approved recurring financial grants, Harold loved his job. When the system changed over to the clerical staff, he resented the change. He and the other social service caseworkers had fought long, hard and brutally to get the clerical staff to do *all* of their written work. They contended that they couldn't service the clients properly because too much time was spent at the desks writing forms for the checks.

State legislation not only assigned writing the checks but many related professional duties to the clerical staff so that the tables were turned on the social staff. Social workers began to resent the Income Maintenance Specialists.

They even helped the clients to create a clients' union, to protest the Income Maintenance staff. The social staff brought cleints to the centers by the busload to make the job more difficult for the IMS staff. But none of the pressures succeeded in removing the IMS staff. They were a rugged crew and the

91

increases in work that the clerical staff received from the changeover just spurred the spunky IMS on to bigger and better goals.

Harold had his own personal reasons for hating the changeover. He had a good thing going with the clients who were on his caseload. Harold was a bachelor and most women found him obnoxious. His persistent use of vulgar language even turned the men off and did not endear him to anybody.

When he found he could use his job as caseworker to intimidate the clients, he got all the sex he wanted.

One of his prime hobbies was reading pornography and watching x-rated movies. He said he considered this healthy and pretended to be shocked at anyone who did not participate. Anybody who called him sick, he labeled as narrow-minded prudes.

Harold's rented furnished room held piles of pornographic material and sexual devices that he ordered from erotic magazines and underground newspapers.

Occasionally, he would bring his movie projector into work, and show the boys in the back room one of his obscene movies.

He had a burning yen to settle down with a woman and thought that Sheba, even though she was Black would make him a good wife. The Black clients whom he went out with usually satisfied him sexually, but the ones that would go with him were as vulgar as he. Harold wanted someone respectable, and very decent.

Unfortunately for Harold, Sheba found him as disgusting as he really was. Filthy, internally and externally, he stank constantly of cheap cigar smoke and dirty clothes. His breath was unbearably loathsome from the cigars and strong foods decaying in between his yellow rotting teeth.

Everytime Harold approached Sheba to try to get her to go out with him, she always changed the conversation to a different topic. After awhile, he got the message. He could see that she made a conscious effort to avoid him entirely. He couldn't understand why, he thought she should feel privileged to have a White man for a husband.

Harold tried to smile at her lovingly, but his smile looked more like an evil leer and his rotten teeth were more prominent than ever. Sheba couldn't stand looking at him, he made her feel queasy. His reputation had put a cloud over him.

Then, to Harold's joy, a new worker, Sandra Millinski, came to work at County Bureau #105. She was a divorcee and looking for a man of her own. Anxiously, Harold approached her for a date and was stunned when she accepted.

The two of them were a steady duo about a year, until Sandra had to go into the hospital for surgery. She had started suffering from gynecological misfunctions and excruciating pains after she started going with Harold. She had let him subject her to all of his sexual devices and she paid heavy dues for her transgressions.

The doctor told her she had developed a rapid cancer and all of her female organs would have to be removed through a total hysterectomy to keep it from spreading to other parts of her body.

The romance with Harold was over when she discovered that he was responsible for her ailments. She was warned by her surgeon that further use of those devices would be fatal for her.

Harold gave up on romance with his co-workers after the breakup with Sandra. As it turned out, he should have given up on romance with the clients, too.

One of his clients came into the center to get moving expenses. She had found a nice apartment with two bedrooms, one for her daughter and one for her. He convinced her to let him move in with her and they shared a bedroom. Harold then felt on top of the world. She kept the house reasonably clean and had his dinner ready at night. He gave her what he was paying for rent before plus some money for food.

Down in County Bureau #105's ABD section, Josephine was sitting, during her lunch hour, at her desk, talking to her specialists, Sylvia, Rita and Anne. They were not too far from caseworker Harold Stein's desk.

A client in her late twenties walked over to them and demanded, "Where's Mr. Stein? I want to see him."

Sylvia, a plump White woman in her fifties, said, "He's out to lunch."

The client gave her a dirty look and walked away.

A few moments later, the client came back and confronted Sylvia.

"You honky, you. You sat on your fat ass and told me Mr. Stein was out to lunch. He was in that back room playing cards. Why don't you get off your fat ass and go to work?"

Sylvia, angered by the client's tone and words, replied, "I don't see you doing anything but collecting welfare checks!"

The other women were trying to get Sylvia to keep her mouth shut. The client was big and tough looking, and on the verge of taking a swing at Sylvia.

"If I wanted to, I could go get an application and sit on my ass too."

"So why the hell don't you?" Sylvia asked sarcastically.

It was fortunate for Sylvia that the client decided not to be bothered with her and kept on walking. Josephine was relieved because there weren't any security guards around to rescue them if help was needed.

****

Robert Dunn sat at his desk staring blankly at the papers in front of him.

He hadn't seen Sheba for weeks. He knew she was in her office and wondered why she hadn't made any attempt to talk to him, even about work. There was always something to discuss, new policies and procedures, etc.

Maybe she was still upset over the death of her only brother.

Well, if she wouldn't come to him, he would go to her. He seldom went to her office, though it was only a short distance away, it was like another world. There were plants on the window sill, the bookcase and the table, which was covered with flowered contact paper. The office was quite cheerful and comfortable.

One of the chairs from the lounge was in her office. On the walls were posters and drawings. Sheba's daughter's drawings dominated one wall. A pleasant feeling surged through Bob and he immediately felt closer to Sheba as he looked around the office.

She looked up at him and smiled happily as he entered the office.

"Hi, Bob!"

"Hi, yourself. Trying to play hard to get?"

"No, why?"

"You haven't been near my office for two weeks."

"I've been busy trying to develop lesson plans for all the new procedures that the Main office inundated us with. There's over 15 and they all have a deadline."

"Too busy to see me?"

"I'm never too busy to see you".

"Whew! Am I glad to hear that!"

He waited for her to answer. When she didn't, he asked. "Well?"

"Well, well, well." She said smiling.

"You know what I'm waiting to hear."

Sheba looked down at her fingernails as if she had never seen them before.

"Sheba, answer me. Will you or won't you have dinner with me?" he asked quietly.

"Bob, I truly want to say yes, but I have mixed feelings."

"Why mixed?"

"It's a long story and it would probably bore you to death."

"Try me." He looked at his watch."It's three o'clock, I'll give you two hours."

She laughed.

"It won't take that long, but maybe you will want to withdraw your offer before I'm finished."

"I doubt it."

"We'll see."

"To begin with I practice total abstinence, I don't believe in premarital or single sex life. <u>No</u> exceptions."

Sheba watched Bob's face to see his reaction to that. His eyes opened wide and his eyebrows shot up.

"I don't drink or smoke, and most people who do seem to have serious problems with that. They tend to try to pressure me into doing the things that they do. Inevitably, I am told things like,'Come on, it won't hurt you', 'Loosen up don't be so uptight', or 'Why are you such a goody-goody', or 'Don't be such a prude'. I've stopped going to parties for that reason. I don't preach to people to stop them from drinking, why should they be so obsessed to try to make me start drinking? I like having my brain as clear as it can be at all times. Live and let live."

"Sheba, I can appreciate what you're telling me. I won't try to force you to drink or do anything you don't want to do." Bob's face and tones were serious.

"Let me finish what I have to say. One of my friends decided that I needed a man desperately. I guess I looked too happy to her. She said that she knew this 'perfectly' marvelous man for me. After she spent a couple of days convincing me he was someone I dare not miss out on, I let her give him my telephone number. Well, he called within the next few days and said he would be over to my house. He didn't bother to ask if it was all right with me. To make matters worse, he came two hours late, at ten o'clock. I had already started getting prepared to go to bed, next day was a work day."

Bob raised his eyebrows, Sheba continued.

"When I opened the door, he swaggered in past me and found his way into the livingroom. I suppose I should be happy that he didn't make his way straight into the bedroom! He was just about the opposite of everything I like in a man, except for one asset, he was clean, physically. His mind was filthy and his lanuage was coarse. Before I showed him out of the door, he made it very clear that he expected to have an ongoing affair. He said he wanted me to be ready for him, no matter what time of day or night he happened to come by my house, even if it was 3am in the morning. What kind of life is that? Do women do that sort of thing?"

Bob looked thoughtful. "I wouldn't know. I never lived that way."

"Well, when my friend heard that I threw him out, she called me "Ms. Goody-two-shoes. She tells everybody that I am just too good to be true."

"Sheba, that man was a sleazebag. If I'd been there, I would have thrown him out for you."

"Gee thanks. I needed that. Most people find my 'laws' of life, spiritually, morally,mentally and physical, too complicated to understand."

"How so?" Bob inquired.

"Because of the choices most people make that lead to unhappiness."

"Why do you say that?"

"They haven't learned to control their emotions. Human beings were created many levels above the lower forms of animal life. The very lowest form of animal life can sleep, get food and shelter for itself and offspring, have sex and children. Life should have more meaning than that for human beings. There should be a compulsion to find deeper and more spiritual realities so that life will be more contented, and no need for any kind of artificial stimulation or non-constructive social behavior." Sheba looked at Bob, expecting him to take wings and fly out if the room with some kind of lame excuse.

"Sheba, love of my life, I understand and agree with every word you said. I can appreciate what you've been through, and I *still* want to take you out. We can simply get to know each other better. On my word of honor, I won't try to rush you into *anything.*"

He wanted to give her time to take that in, so he reached inside his jacket pocket for his pipe and tobacco. His movements were slow and deliberate as he filled his pipe.

Looking thoughtful, Sheba said, "Well, you know better than I do what your intentions are. I just don't want you wasting your time and money."

"Why would it be a waste?"

"If your intentions are 'honorable', then I suppose you would not consider the evening a waste."

Bob lit his pipe, in spite of the sign in Sheba's office that read "Thank you for not smoking" and took a long drag. Letting the smoke out slowly to hide his sigh of relief. That sounded promising.

"Okay are you finished lecturing me? Now will you answer my question? Will you or won't you have dinner with me? Woman, I can not take much more of this suspense. Answer me. No more if s, and s, or but s. Pronto!"

Sheba laughed heartily.

"Okay Bob. I will have dinner with you."

He took another long drag from his pipe as he gazed into her eyes dreamily.

"I'll call you at home tonight and we'll make plans, okay?"

"I'll look forward to hearing from you."

Neither Bob nor Sheba noticed Pearl, who was lurking outside the door, listening to every word they spoke. She waited until Bob left, then ran to spread the latest gossip.

When Bob got back to his office, Raphael, the patrolman, was in the outer office waiting for him, with Willie and a young employee, named Sheldon.

Raphael spoke first to Bob.

"Mr Dunn, we have a problem here." Raphael was holding Willie by the arm.

"Come into my office."

Bob knocked the tobacco ashes out of his pipe into an ashtray, and took his chair behind the desk.

"Now, have a seat everybody."

Willie and Sheldon sat down, Raphael remained standing.

"Where do we begin, Raphael?"

"Willie borrowed Sheldon's bike at lunch time. While Willie was out riding, he said three guys threatened to kill him if he didn't give them the bike."

Bob made Willie repeat the story. It seemed to him that Willie was lying, but there was no way to prove this.

"Well, Willie, what are you going to do about it?"

"What do you mean?"

"I mean Sheldon is out of a bike. How much did the bike cost, Sheldon?"

"One hundred and thirty dollars."

"That's a lot of money, Willie. How are you going to reimburse Sheldon?"

"Reimburse?

"Well, do you have any witnesses to back up your story?" Bob asked.

"No." Willie looked down at the floor.

"Then if we call the police, they'd probably charge *you* with the robbery."

Willie looked worried. He had some dope in his pocket, the cops might search him. Then they would question him and he might end up telling them he sold the bike to get the dope.

"Look, Mr. Dunn, would it be all right if I paid Sheldon a little at a time out of my pay?"

"Don't ask me, ask Sheldon."

"Is that all right with you, Sheldon?" Willie asked meekly.

"I don't know, Mr Dunn. Willie splits every payday after he gets his check."

"Look man, I'll give your money to Mr. Dunn, okay?"

Bob looked at Sheldon, who really did not go for that deal.

"Raphael, would you be willing to escort Willie and Sheldon to the bank on paydays?"

"If it will help Sheldon, Mr. Dunn."

"Okay then, the next two or three paychecks, you give Sheldon fifty or sixty dollars. I'll hold your paycheck until Raphael comes to my office."

"Yes sir, anything you say, sir."

It was five o'clock when they finally left, Bob got his attache case and went home.

Two days later, Willie was back in Bob's office. This time Raphael and J.C. another patrolman brought him in, in handcuffs.

"Mr. Dunn, Willie just stabbed a worker on the third floor."

Bob was fighting to keep his cool. He did manage to say calmly, "Did you call the police?

"Yes, sir," J.C. answered.

"Three other patrolmen are with Alphonso, waiting for an ambulance, and a patrol car." Raphael said.

"What's the story *this* time?" Bob looked at Raphael.

"Willie's in the drug pushing racket now. He ran out of marijuana today and substituted oregano. Alphonso bought a few joints. Alphonso smoked some of it and nearly doubled up. He went back to Willie and started to beat him, Willie pulled out his knife and cut him."

At that moment, an officer walked in Bob's office. Raphael repeated the story to them. They took notes and Willie away with them.

With a few moments of peace on his hands, Bob looked dreamily out the window and recalled his telephone conversation with Sheba two nights ago. He'd had the devil's own time waiting until the right time to call her. At eight o'clock promptly her phone rang.

Sheba's daughter, Donna, answered the phone on the second ring, and called her to the phone.

"Ma, it's for you." He heard Donna declare.

After a few seconds, Sheba picked up the phone.

"Hello?" Her voice was musical and sent pleasant vibrations through his body.

"Hi, love. This is Bob."

"Bob, your voice sounds so nice over the phone, so deep and throaty."

"Nicer than in person?"

"No. It's just that I can concentrate fully on your voice, when you're not around to distract me."

"The feelings are mutual, you've got quite a sexy voice yourself."

"I bet you say that to all your dates."

"Sure, why not? By the way, when and where is our dinner date going to be?"

Sheba thought for a second.

"I'll leave that up to you, Bob."

"I want to please you."

"You've got to remember, you're the man about town. I'm the lady who rarely goes out on dates. I'm hardly a connoisseur of restaurants."

"I know just the place. Do you like seafood?"

"Shrimp, lobster, Southern fried whitings and butterfish, not much else."

"They've got all that and more. What time and what day?"

"Early, very early on Saturday. I get hungry early. Fact is, I usually eat about two on Saturdays and fill up for the rest of the day. But I'll eat lunch this time and wait until five."

"I can pick you up at two if you like."

"No, I don't want to spoil your plans."

"Far from it. I'll have more time to spend with you."

"Sir you are a gentleman as well as a scholar. But I'll look forward to seeing you at five o'clock. That will give me some time to take care of household chores."

He stayed on the phone with her until eleven o'clock that night, something he hadn't done since he was a teenager. His thoughts were so filled with her that he dreamed about her all night long.

The next day at work, he visited her office early in the morning, while she was watering her plants.

"Good morning, love of my life, I dreamed about you all last night." Bob was very happy.

"Oh? I wonder if we dreamed the same dream." They smiled at each other.

He walked close to her and put his arm around her, she in turn, put her arm around him. They stood like that for a few moments gazing into each other's eyes and were startled by Pearl's voice, speaking in harsh, acidic tones.

"May I speak to you in your office, Mr.Dunn? It's very important."

Bob and Sheba looked at each other, and Sheba could feel her face blushing hotly. Of all people to walk in, it would have to be her. Pearl never got to work this early when she was in Sheba's ABD unit.

Bob didn't seem to be upset at all. He excused himself and went back to his office with Pearl.

On the way to Bob's office, Pearl was burning with jealousy. She hated Sheba's guts, particularly because of the days when she worked under Sheba's supervision. Pearl had not been used to putting in a good day's work and Sheba put a kink in her office social life at that time.

Now she worked as a supervisor in a section of accounting, after passing a County exam. This section disbursed the emergency checks and some petty cash to the clients. She was in the throes of a terrible problem down there.

Once in Bob's office, he offered her a chair. Pearl fluttered her false eyelashes at him and rolled her eyes in what she thought was an appealing manner.

Bob cleared his throat to keep from laughing out loud at her rolling those huge, cowlike eyes.

"Miss Boone, what seems to be the problem?"

"Someone is stealing money from the cash box. Also a number of blank checks are missing."

"What? Do you have any idea who the thief is?"

"Yes. I think it's two people working together. Andrea and Bobbie. Andrea is our typist who types out the checks. Bobbie is the messenger who brings the cash and blank checks from the main office."

"Well, first we'll have to put tighter security controls on the cash and checks. The main office will have to be notified and the numbers on the blank checks will have to be tightly controlled. Do you have the numbers of the missing checks?"

"I have the girls checking out all of the carbon copies of checks issued through the office now."

"Good. I'll call you up to my office this afternoon. The office manager and assistant office managers will be here and we'll map out the necessary strategy."

Pearl left, but not without giving him one last flutter of her false eyelashes, then twisting her rear end provocatively.

Immediately after Pearl left, Josephine came into his office.

"Mr. Dunn," Josephine's shrill voice was nervous, "I've got to get Leroy out of my group."

"Calm down, Josephine. What's Leroy doing to upset you?"

"Plenty. He comes strolling in everyday after ten o'clock and someone is clocking him in at nine. He takes three hours for lunch if he decides to work for the day. When he doesn't want to work all day, he just disappears. But someone clocks him out. He never gets docked on his check, even though he shouldn't have any annual or sick leave. Sometimes I'm glad when he doesn't come back from lunch. He always gets high after lunch, and when he's high, he's mean."

"Have you talked to him?"

"Yes. I've talked to him until I'm blue in the face."

"Is he in now?"

"Yes."

"Send him up to my office. I'll speak to him."

"Couldn't you take him out of my group?"

"That won't solve anything."

"But he won't listen to me."

"Josephine, you have to assert yourself as a supervisor. There is a disciplinary procedure that is mandated by law. If Leroy is doing everything you say he is doing, then you must follow the proper procedures in order to remove him from your unit. The man is not capable of functioning anywhere."

Two days later, Leroy was caught forging checks. He had cashed approximately twenty-five hundred dollars worth of checks. His friend Bobbie had stolen over a thousand blank checks.

Both Leroy and Bobbie disappeared from the County Bureau #105. Someone had tipped them off that the district attorney was out to get them. Andrea also became hard to find.

Bob had found himself caught up in many crisis in the two days since he called Sheba. Today was Friday, tomorrow was Saturday, the big day.

The three of them, Leroy, Andrea, and Bobbie, had had a good racket going. Bobbie would steal the blank checks, Leroy would make up phony check approval forms with a fictitious client's name, number and address, Andrea would type the checks, Leroy cashed them, and the money was split three ways.

Bobbie and Leroy shot up on heroin in the supply room. The late Duke had started both of them on their habit. When Duke died, the price went sky high, there were no more bargains.

There were at least ten young men hooked on drugs at County Bureau #105. Duke had really pushed his wares. He would start them out by giving them free joints for awhile. When the kicks wore down, he would give them one or two shots of the hard stuff. He felt that the choice to use or not to use drugs was each individual's responsibility.

They could always say "no." He was merely the seller of goods they wanted to buy. If they didn't buy from him, they would buy from someone else.

Josephine didn't have to worry about Leroy working in her unit anymore. The police found a stack of the blank checks in his desk drawer. They caught the three of them, two weeks later, trying to leave Mega City in Leroy's 1967 Chevrolet.

****

Edith was pretending to be working at her desk when Bob's secretary brought in the new assistant office manager from the main office. Her eyes nearly popped put of her head as the shapely red head walked casually into her office.

"I'm Patricia Harris, assistant office manager. I was assigned from the main office." Patricia's voice cooed sexily at Edith.

Edith's eyes took in all of Patricia, her jersey blouse clinging to her full breasts and the pants so close-fit that they showed every curve.

"I'm so happy to meet you, Miss Harris." Edith's face was now beaming. She would have Patricia working close to her, now that she saw her.

At that moment, Sidney walked into the office and Edith introduced them. He, too, appreciated the way Patricia looked but he didn't comment because he knew Edith would be jealous.

The assignment that Edith gave Patricia was on another floor and they rarely saw each other at first. Then Edith got one of her buddies to invite Patricia to a drink-in in the supply room. Patricia accepted and drank more than anyone there, except Edith.

Patricia became a regular in the supply room, as well as Edith's friend, fortunately for her. It soon became apparent that the assignment given to Patricia was too much for her to handle. Since she was hardly ever at work, she wasn't able to learn the job or keep her subordinates under control.

That section was falling apart and Bob Dunn was pressuring Edith to take Patricia out of there and replace her. Edith was afraid Mr. Dunn would transfer Patricia out of County Bureau #105 if she didn't find something Patricia could handle. Patricia was just beginning to come around to Edith's way of thinking and she didn't want to lose her now.

Edith shifted Sidney and Patricia. Now Patricia's office was right across from her and she could see Patricia every time she went in or out of her office.

Patricia had a vague idea that Edith might be homosexual, but Edith's relationships puzzled her. Besides Sidney, there were several other men who would take Edith home when she wasn't driving her little Volkswagon. When she got too drunk, someone else would drive her home. Each man behaved as if he was her one and only lover.

Patricia, meanwhile, due to her excessive drinking, was having dizzy spells and hallucinations.

She was standing in her livingroom one evening, dusting the furniture, when she thought she saw the form of a man coming out of the kitchen. She grew frightened and called her great dane, Bullet.

Usually, Bullet would come bounding towards her when she called his name. This day, he came of the bedroom, cautiously, and backed up whining.

Patricia stood rooted to the spot, as the form of the man turned into a mist-like cloud, and moved slowly towards her. The mist surrounded her and she fought it furiously before falling to the floor and blacking out.

She didn't know how long she lay there, but she decided to consult a medium to find out what happened.

The next day, Patricia stayed home from work, and went to see Madame Zahara.

Madame Zahara really could not help Patricia, but since Patricia was not aware of that fact, Madame Zahara decided to take her money.

"The mist means there is someone who hates you. Nothing is supposed to penetrate your aura. We each have an aura surrounding us. Somehow the strong hatred of someone with a strong will has managed to do this to you."

Madame Zahara went into the back of the room, and came back with a tiny brown envelope she handed to Patricia.

"Take this, put it under the chair or table where the person sits all the time, who you think hates you for any reason. My fee is fourty dollars."

Patricia paid her.

Inside the envelope were dried up cockroaches and tiny pieces of twigs all crumbled up to look mysterious and cabalistic.

The first person Patricia thought of was her boyfriend's wife. She had tried to hurt Patricia and William in many ways. But that was over a year ago and William said she was going out with someone else.

William had a franchise for an ice cream store. Patricia would go there in the evenings and help until he closed up at night. He was a big, husky, Black man, 50 years old, but could pass for thirty-five. He kept Patricia in shape, teaching her how to swim, play tennis and ski. Sometimes he would let the help run the store while they went away on the weekend. When he found out that they took more money than he made, he would just close the store when he and Patricia went away.

William did not believe in the occult so when Patricia talked to him about the incident, he shrugged off what she said. He was worried about her dizzy spells and all-too-frequent hallucinations.

The day she came back to work, Patricia consulted with Edith. She told her all about the incident and what the medium had said.

Edith, sensing her chance to get closer to Patricia as well as a chance to turn Patricia against Sheba, pretended she was trying to help her.

"You know, Patricia, I think Sheba hates you. The rumor is she and the director have a thing going. But I've seen the way he looks at you even when Sheba is around and she is a very jealous woman."

Patricia's face brightened. She was very much aware of her own attractiveness and susceptible to Edith's lies. Besides, she was attracted to Bob Dunn. Prior to now, she didn't think she had any hope to ever be with him. She had worked in the main office when he was there and he'd never given her a tumble. Maybe he never had a chance to take a good look at her before.

The small brown envelope was clutched in her hand as she headed for Sheba's office. The blame had to be laid on somebody and Patricia herself would be the last person in the world responsible. Rather than believe she was psychotic or suffering from drunken delusions, she accepted the stories that let someone else's emotions control her.

Arriving at Sheba's office, Patricia was disappointed to see Sheba at her desk working.

"Hello, Patricia, can I help you?" Sheba questioned with a puzzled look on her face. Patricia had never come into her office before and since Edith did not care for her, she assumed, Patricia had been influenced by Edith's feelings.

"Hi, Sheba." Smiling her brightest, phoniest smile, Patricia sat in the chair closest to the desk. "Could you tell me where I can find the State letters?"

While she waited for Sheba to answer, she leaned forward, pretending to fix her shoes and threw the envelope under Sheba's desk.

Sheba saw the movement and when Patricia left, she picked up the envelope and examined it's contents. She promptly headed to Patricia's office.

Glancing toward Edith's office, Sheba saw both Edith and Patricia in deep conversation. She quickly threw the envelope under Patricia's desk and left.

Saturday finally came!

When the doorbell rang promptly at five o'clock, Donna, Sheba's teenage daughter, rushed to the door. She was burning with curiousity to see what type of man her mother was going out with.

Donna had her own bevy of boyfriends. They kept the phone busy and Sheba had to put a curfew on the time of night they could call her. Otherwise, neither Sheba or Donna would have been able to get any sleep.

"Who is it?" Donna asked from her side of the peephole in the door.

"Bob Dunn." He felt his pulse quicken.

Donna unlocked all four locks.

Bob walked inside the apartment, his eyes searching for Sheba. He looked at Donna, and knew immediately who she was, no question about it, this girl was Sheba's daughter.

"Hello, Donna, I'm Bob Dunn."

"Hello, Mr. Dunn. My mother will be right out. Won't you have a seat?"

"Thank you."

The apartment was homey and comfortable, the sofa, big and super soft. He sank down among the cushions.

Donna was trying to keep her cool and give Bob the impression that she was a very hip young lady.

"Can I get you anything? The strongest drink we keep in the house is sweet Kosher wine."

Bob smiled broadly at that.

"I 'm well aware of your mother's tastes. By the way, I've seen your drawings in your mother's office. You are quite a talented young lady."

"Thank you. I'll see what's keeping her."

She walked casually out of the living room, but when she got out of range of Bob's vision, she ran into her mother's bedroom and bounced on the bed.

"Ma! Why didn't you tell me he was so tall and good looking? He's bad, very bad."

"Bad? I thought you just said he was good looking."

"Well, bad means good."

Sheba raised her eyebrows."I'm glad you like him. How do you like my outfit?"

"You look beautiful, Ma!" Donna always gave her the straight story. If Sheba did not look all right, then Donna would have hinted that she should have worn something else.

The outfit that Sheba had on was her own design, custom made by her own hands. She had majored in fashion design and dressmaking in high school. At that time, work in that field was scarce for Black fashion designers, so Sheba had turned to civil service for ready employment.

The top was a burnished gold, with mandarin collar, dolman sleeves and handkerchief hemline. With it, she wore black velvet pants, high-heeled sandals of gold and carried a small black velvet bag, which she'd also made.

Sheba combed her hair up, in the 'Parisian' hairstyle that Alfred Greene, one of her former clients, had complimented.

A last-minute touch of a perfume that cost fifty dollars an ounce, which she traveled far to get at discount prices, and she was ready.

Sheba said to Donna "be good" and went down the hall to greet Bob. She was as excited as a school girl going on her first date.

She prayed to herself on the way. Please, GOD, don't let anything go wrong tonight.

When she reached the living room, Bob got up from the sofa and gave a long whistle, then said, "Wow", very softly.

She gave him the once over and said "Wow yourself", softly.

His navy blue suit was tailored just for him, with the lapels and pockets handstitched. Bob's black shoes shone like the midnight sun. He had obviously gone to the barber shop that very day, because he looked excellent. His shaving lotion was near aphrodisiac. The vibrations shooting through both of them almost irresistable.

It was a long drive out to the Ocean View restaurant, but it turned out to be worthwhile.

Once there and seated at the table, they only had eyes for each other. Neither finished the meal, although they spent nearly three hours in the restaurant.

Before they started back, they walked along the boardwalk, holding hands, talking for hours. It was one o'clock in the morning when Bob realized he had better start the long drive back to Sheba's place. At her door, she invited him in for a minute before his long drive back home. Bob lived on the island with his parents.

Bob looked down at her and said, "I'm not sure I'll be able to restrain myself."

"Well, if that's the case…" She started to close the door in his face.

"Wait a minute, I'll come in for a minute. I'll be good."

She let him walk by her into the living room. Only the foyer light was on as she started to pass him to turn on a brighter lamp.

He pulled her to him gently and put his arms around her, pressing her close to him. They were both burning up with desire for each other. Sheba felt Bob's breath hot on her face even before their lips met. The heat from his lips matched hers and they were both transported into a state of ecstasy.

They stood there kissing passionately, oblivious to the rest of the world, until Donna's voice startled them.

"Oh, I'm sorry, Ma. I thought I heard you come in, but I checked your room and you weren't there." She turned and left the room quickly, a little embarrassed at finding her mother in Bob's arms.

Sheba pulled away from Bob.

"It's Sunday already, Bob. We'd better say goodnight or good morning."

He kissed her again, then reluctantly let her go.

"I'll call you this evening, love."

Bob left, wanting to stay.

Later, Sheba was in bed, trying to sleep, she realized that she had fallen in love with Bob. It had been coming on slowly for the past six months, since first meeting him, and she could not ignore his obvious feelings for her. She liked everything about that magnificent man, his attitude, his looks, their mutual respect and most importantly he seemed to care for her very much. Otherwise, how else could he put up with all the restraints she brought to him?

At the office, he had spoiled her rotten, even though she still worked very hard to please him. Sheba thought she might never be satisfied working for someone else.

After finally falling asleep, she was awakened by the delicious smell of beef stewing. Donna was cooking dinner. Sheba glanced at the clock, it was noon. Her thoughts went to Bob again.

Last night had been so wonderful and exciting that she was thankful to GOD for answering her prayers.

Bob called her as promised that evening and they made plans for the next weekend.

Even before he made the call to Sheba, he had spoken to his parents about her. He had known almost immediately after meeting Sheba that he loved her. His decision to marry her had been made last night, during their long walk and illuminating conversation. He'd never met anyone like her before. They had talked about a wide variety of subjects, including themselves, and still he felt as though they could go on talking forever.

He slept later than usual, and missed going to church with his parents. It wasn't the first time, but he had a lot to be thankful for now.

Dinner was early on Sundays, and as they sat around the dinner table, he figured he might as well break the good news.

"Mom, Dad. I want to get married."

"Do you have someone special in mind, son?" His father looked happy.

"Yes. Sheba."

"After just one date?" His mother questioned.

"It's much more than that. I see her every day at work. We're together a lot at the office, constantly consulting each other on departmental policies and procedures. Remember, we've known each other for over six months."

"When are we going to meet her?" His father asked.

"Would you like to invite her and her daughter to dinner?" Bob asked them.

His mother answered, "That would be fine son, make the arrangements with her. We'll go along with whatever date you decide."

"Okay. Mom, now I just have to propose to her."

His parents looked at each other.

"If she says yes, where will you live?"

"I don't know, Dad. I guess I'll have to buy a house somewhere. Maybe I can find one like this."

"Why not this house?"

"I doubt if she would want to impose upon you and Mom."

"We've been thinking about living in our house in Texas, but we didn't want to leave you here alone. But once you are married, we'll be free to go."

"You could have gone, Dad. You shouldn't have let me stop you."

"Son, we love you, and you weren't stopping us. It's just that we wanted you to have someone here with you who loved you."

"Well, start making preparations."

"We want to be here for the wedding."

"You can always come back here or I'll convince Sheba to go there and we can honeymoon in Texas."

Bob knew his parents had property in Texas. That's where they all vacationed, every year. It was beautiful there, 20 acres of prime land that his grandfather had left to his mother. The house was filled with beautiful pieces of furniture, also inherited by his mother. On the adjoining land were close relatives, with homes every bit as warm and lovely as Bob's parents.

His mother said they would wait until Sheba accepted Bob's proposal before the move.

At the office the next morning, Bob waited in Sheba's office until she arrived.

She didn't think it was possible, but when he kissed her that morning, it was even more passionate than the day before.

"If you keep that up, you'll have me getting here at the crack of dawn," she said breathlessly.

"If I keep this up, I might not even bother to go home."

While he held her in his arms he said, "I love you more than I have ever loved anyone before in my life.

It's impossible to imagine living the rest of my life without you. Please say that you will marry me."

"I dreamed all last night that you had proposed to me and we were married."

"You didn't answer my question. Will you marry me?"

She kissed him.

"Woman, answer me! Are you trying to play hard to get?"

"Yes. Yes. Yes!"

"Three yesses!"

"Yes, I am playing hard to get and yes, yes, I will marry you."

"My mom and dad would like to have you and Donna over for dinner one day soon. It's up to you to set the date."

"For the wedding?"

"Yes and for the dinner. They want to give us the house. Mom and Dad want to live in Texas where they were both born. Mom owns a house and land there."

"Bob, are you sure we won't be putting them out?" Sheba went to her desk.

"No, they had already made plans to go there."

He told her about the conversation he had had with his parents, then they set a date for the dinner and a tentative date for the wedding.

Grinning, Bob returned to his office, finding Evelyn Coburn, newly assigned Head Supervisor of the filing section, waiting for him there.

She was on the verge of tears.

"Jimmie threatened to kill me."

Startled, Bob questioned her further.

"Start from the beginning."

"Jimmie and Alphonso disappear every day about the same time. I've spoken to them so often I feel crazy. Each time I speak to Jimmie, he is insubordinate and insulting. They don't want to work, even when they are at their desks. Friday, I followed them to see if they leave the building."

"Did they leave the building?"

"No. They went downstairs to the first aid room. I waited a while and I got Raphael to come with me to see what they were doing in there."

"What were they doing?"

"I think they had just taken some dope."

"What? Why did you think that?" Bob felt drained. 'What in the hell was going on in the place?' he thought to himself.

"There was a syringe and some other things on the table."

"Were there any drugs around?"

"No. Jimmie asked me 'what the hell do you want?' and when Raphael chased them out of there to go back to work, that's when he threatened me."

"This was Friday?"

"Yes."

"Why did you wait until today?"

"I was frightened."

"Aren't you frightened now?"

"Yes I am, even more. Mr.Dunn, he really means to kill me."

"I'm sure it's just talk, Mrs. Coburn. Even if we called the police, I doubt they could do anything."

"I found this in one of the file cabinet drawers little while ago."

She took a pistol out of a manila envelope and laid it on Bob's desk.

Bob called the police immediately. When the officers came, they examined the pistol.

"He couldn't kill anybody with this pistol, it won't fire. We'll take him and the pistol to the precinct for questioning. This is dangerous harassment."

Evelyn was still frightened and pleaded with Bob to transfer her to another bureau immediately, Jimmie could always get a gun that worked. He belonged to a gang called the Stoneheads, who were rumored to have murdered one of the social staff at County Bureau #105.

Reportedly, one of the Eligibility Specialists, Celestine Carson, a tall, husky but attractive Black woman was going with a female case supervisor who was making a good salary. Celestine's salary wasn't half her friend's. Her friend gave her large amounts of money, which helped to support Celestine's three children. She was a dedicated worker and utilized everything she learned at Sheba's training sessions.

Once, Sheba happened to be the floor when Celestine had a disagreeable client who was threatening her. Celestine stood up, according to Sheba's instructions, and kept her hand on the staple gun to be able to ward off any blows the client might try to inflict upon her. Standing up helped to keep her at an advantage.

Fortunately, the client did not get physical. Celestine had a serious look on her face most of the time that Sheba admired. It reminded her of the serious look that her mother used to have on her face, the look that said, "don't hand me any crap."

That's why no one was more shocked when Celestine took off for parts unknown, because she had involved herself in a lesbian triangle. The core of the problem was the social worker and her habit of giving large sums of money to her lovers.

Before getting involved with Celestine, the woman, Lydia Bailey, had a teenaged lover. The girl had a brother in the Stoneheads who had a reputation for the bodies they left behind. Lydia met the girl during a summer youth program when the girl worked in the center.

After Lydia decided to dump the girl and took up with Celestine, she was warned by the girl to break off with Celestine and take her back. Lydia ignored the warnings and a week later she was found murdered in her bed, with nothing on. The girl had convinced Lydia to make love to her one last time. While Lydia waited for the girl to come out of the bathroom, the girl opened the front door and let her brother and his friends into the apartment.

After hearing that story, Bob called the main office and apprised them of the situation. Evelyn was given an immediate transfer and her whereabouts were kept confidential. Not even Bob knew where she was transferred. Evelyn simply went to the main office one day and was not seen again at County Bureau #105.

A call from the main office to Bob requested that he have Barbara Grover, one of the workers from the second floor, come to the main office. She was found to be fraudulently collecting welfare checks.

Bob sent his secretary down to tell her he would like to speak to her as soon as she was free.

Barbara was interviewing two clients, a small Italian woman and her 14 year old daughter.

"I'll be up as soon as I've finished here". Barbara told the secretary.

She turned back to her clients, addressing the mother.

"Mrs. Marconi, when was your daughter's baby born?"

"One week ago."

"Isn't this a little early to bring your daughter into the center? She just had the baby, maybe she isn't well enough to do this now."

"She's a tough girl, she can take it. Ever since she was 12 years old, she's been running around. I couldn't do nothing with her."

"Why didn't you come in before the baby was born? We would have given you an extra allowance then."

"I didn't know she was pregnant until she gave birth."

Barbara looked at the little skinny teenager, and wondered how anybody could not know this child was pregnant.

"Mrs. Maroni, if your daughter was running around since she was 12 years old, why didn't you take her to family planning?"

"My religion forbids us to use contraceptives."

Barbara didn't argue with her, just continued interviewing the clients and gathering the necessary information. When the interview was over she went to Bob's office.

He was talking to someone, so she waited until he was free.

"Come in Barbara. Have a seat."

Barbara was puzzled. Bob saw this but he couldn't reassure her.

"Barbara, I received a call from the main office. I'm not going to try to soft-pedal the matter, the problem is quite serious. They are in touch with Special Investigations and are ready to report you to the District Attorney's office for prosecution."

Barbara looked frightened.

"Why, Mr. Dunn?"

"Are you on welfare now?'

"Yes, but they know I'm working. My salary is figured into my budget."

"Did you ever own a home?"

"Yes. My husband was with me then."

"Did you apply for welfare at that time?"

"After he walked out on me. I wasn't working and welfare was the only way I could take care of my eight children."

"You have eight children?"

"Yes. I had my first child when I was fifteen and didn't stop until my husband walked out on me."

"Why didn't you tell the Department that you owned the house?"

"It was just a shack, but it was all we had. My friends said the Department would take it away from me."

"Do you still have the house?"

"No. It burned down two years ago."

"Well, the Department wants the money you concealed from them."

"What money? I didn't sell the house, it burned down."

"You and your husband had the house insured for twenty thousand dollars. The insurance company states that they paid the claim one month after the house burned down."

Barbara was shocked.

"Mr Dunn, they didn't pay it to me. My children and I were lucky to escape with our lives. I would like to know who got that money myself."

"Where was your husband at the time?"

"I don't know. He said he was going down to his family in Florida."

"You can explain all of this to the main office in the morning. The D A's office will investigate to see whose signature is on the check. I would advise you to be on time tomorrow, they will be waiting for you. A representative from the DA's office will be there. If your husband signed the check without your knowledge, which is fraud, he may have also set the house on fire."

"That means he was trying to kill us." Barbara was really upset now.

"If that's true, he's the one in big trouble, not you. Just answer their questions and tell the truth."

"I hope so. I don't have any money to give them. The little money I get goes too fast as it is, there's never enough money to buy food and clothes for myself and the children. With eight children, life can be very hard."

"I know Barbara, but right now, we've got to figure a way to keep you from going to jail. It would be even worse if that happened."

Barbara started crying. Bob noted that he had seen a lot of tears since he was assignd this position. He called the main office back to see if there was any way to work the matter out to everyone's satisfaction.

Their reply was that they would have to take a percentage of Barbara's pay until the entire amount was paid off. But first Barbara would have to go for a hearing until a definite decision could be made.

Bob felt sympathetic and promised to follow up on the matter. Her appointment was for the next morning and she had to be there. She was extemely agitated when she left his office.

On the way back to her desk, she ran into Sidney, Edith's boyfriend. He saw that Barbara was extremely upset and was about to ask her what was wrong when Odessa came down the hall.

Unknown to Edith, Sidney and Odessa had a longstanding affair. It began eight years ago, when Odessa was only 18 years old and Sidney was in his late 40's. He got her pregnant and she had a son, who was now 7 years old. The son strongly resembled Sidney.

When she left the office to give birth, she told everyone she was going to attend college full time. After the baby was born, she came back to work, explaining thst she could not afford day college.

Sidney contributed what he could to support the baby and they continued their affair. But now, Odessa was careful not to get pregnant again.

When mini-skirts were in their full glory, Odessa's dresses were so short that her girdle showed even when she didn't bend over.

She stopped wearing them so short after two men cornered her in an isolated part of the building. One of them started to rip her clothes off. She managed to scream, and Rafael and J.C. rushed to her rescue. The two men got away before they could be identified or apprehended.

But now, Sidney let Barbara go on her way and stopped to talk to Odessa.

"Hi, baby," Sidney was trying to sound hip, young and Black.

"Hi." Odessa treated him coolly since he'd started messing around with Edith.

"What's the matter, baby?"

"Don't baby me. You know what's the matter. I hear your AC-DC girlfriend dumped you for a woman."

"Aw, come on, she's not my girlfriend."

"You come on. Tell me, does she do it like other women?"

"I'll come to your house and explain everything."

Odessa didn't say anything. She was thinking it over. Someone had stolen the keys out of her purse last week. By the time she got home, most of her furniture was gone. Maybe she could get Sidney to come up with enough money to replace some of the furniture.

"Okay, but come early. I have to get my rest." Odessa answered.

Sidney didn't have to worry anymore about Edith seeing him with Odessa. Patricia was apparently doing whatever it was Edith wanted. Sidney walked Odessa to the elevator then he went on his way.

****

<u>1984</u>

The Anonymous Letter

When Pearl heard that Sheba and Bob were engaged, she burned up with jealousy, even though she had a husband of her own at home. Her flirting with Bob had amounted to nothing. As she thought about his reaction to her when she tried to tease him, she felt humiliated. At the time, though, she'd thought it was working.

That bitch Sheba always landed on her feet, Pearl thought, and seemed to get the best of everything. Well this was one man Sheba was not going to get, Pearl would make sure of that.

At break time, Pearl, Rachel and Patricia sat in a corner of the lounge together.

"I'm gonna fix that bitch Sheba. You girls want to help me?"

"Mr. Dunn already gave me one warning and I'm not going to risk losing my job. He was pretty nice when I started all that shit about Shirley," Rachel declared she was turning over a new leaf.

Patricia still had it in for Sheba and when Rachel refused to help Pearl, Patricia volunteered her services.

"I'll help you, she gets on my nerves."

Rachel sucked her teeth loudly.

"Gets on your nerves, my ass. You were mad because Rafael was still chasing after her even when he had already screwed you. Besides, you and Pearl are breathing heavy over Bob Dunn. You ain't kiddin' nobody."

Pearl, upset because Rachel had seen through her game, snarled at Rachel, "Bitch, one of these days I'm gonna' whip your dilapidated ass. You can believe that."

"Any time you are ready." Rachel looked menacingly at Pearl.

Patricia looked at Pearl, waiting for her reaction to Rachel's response, Pearl had not expected Rachel to call her bluff. Both women were waiting to see if she was all talk and no action.

Pearl decided to ignore Rachel.

Rachel figured by Pearl's silence that she wasn't going to do a damn thing and went about the business of eating her lunch.

"What do you want me to do?" Patricia asked Pearl.

"At two-thirty, meet me by Sheba's office. I want you to talk to her for awhile, then tell her that I am down in the back room, screwing Mr. Dunn. She probably won't believe you, so convince her to come on down and see for herself.

Rachel sneered at Pearl.

"How the hell you gonna' get Mr. Dunn to screw you?"

"I'm gonna tell him that Patricia blacked out and is still unconscious and I can't find anybody to take care of her. He always rushes out of his office whenever there is an emergency."

"Then what?" Patricia asked.

"You keep Sheba there until we come out of the room. That's all she has to see, is me comin' out of that back room with her man. He won't be her man anymore. She knows very well what goes on in that back room, everybody knows. That's why you never see her go in there."

"You sure must have it in for her." Patricia said.

"She thinks she's better than everybody else. Won't drink, won't smoke, won't screw anybody, at least not before Mr. Dunn came here. I'll bet she's even making him wait, and he's gonna marry her."

"So? What are you so worried about?" Rachel snapped. "It's her ass!"

"I'm not talking to you. Mind your own business." Pearl answered.

"You got some damned nerve. Telling me to mind my own business, and here you are tryin' get into Sheba's business and Mr.Dunn's life."

Pearl rose to go and Patricia followed her out of the lunch room.

Promptly at 2:30, Patricia went into Sheba's office, after she watched Pearl rush excitedly into Bob's office.

"Mr. Dunn, Patricia passed out and she's unconscious downstairs in the back room. I don't know what to do to help her. Please come down and help me."

Without questioning her further, Bob told his secretary where he was going and hurried out with Pearl. When they got there Pearl closed the door behind them.

Bob looked around the room.

"Where is she?"

"Oh, she must have come to when I left to get you. I tried to find some security guards, but they were all busy somewhere else, so I went up to your office."

"We'll have to try to find her, something serious could be wrong with her."

As he came out of the back room with Pearl, she made an elaborate gesture to straighten out her clothing, patting her hair into place.

Just then, Bob looked across the room, straight into Sheba's eyes, he smiled at her, but she seemed upset about something. She turned her back on him and walked away.

He stood there for a minute or so, puzzled, not noticing that Pearl had taken hold of his arm possessively. Then he saw Patricia.

She looked all right to him, but he walked over to her to check her out.

"What happened, Patricia?" he asked, concerned.

"It's nothing really, Mr. Dunn. About once a month, I get terrible cramps. Pearl thought I fainted, but I get that way for a few moments, that's all."

"Are you sure you are all right?"

"Yes, I'm sure."

Bob left her and went up to Sheba's office, to find out why she had behaved so strangely. She wasn't in her office, he decided to wait until she returned. Her jacket and purse were still there, which meant she was coming back.

It was 3:30 when he sat down to wait at 4:44 he was worried when she still hadn't returned. He went looking for her.

Bob didn't know Sheba had seen him in her office and was deliberately staying away. She was really hurting.

When she saw him come out of that dreadful back room with Pearl, her eyes had flooded with tears and even her heart seemed to hurt.

Sheba hurried into the ladies' room and locked herself in one of the booths. She cried silently for what seemed to be ages.

She just couldn't stop crying. This was the second time a man at County Bureau #105 had hurt her and this time, the pain was deeper and tearing her insides and head apart. She was grateful for one thing, she was spared the sight of catching him in the act.

Yesterday, Sunday, she was ecstatically happy. The three of them, Donna, Bob and

herself were painting Bob's house. They were doing this on weekends. They had something in mind for all nine rooms.

The spacious attic was going to be Donna's studio. The light in there was wonderful for an artist, also it would be a sewing room for Donna. Sheba and Bob would each have a den with wood-paneled walls and plenty of bookshelves. As for the three largest bedrooms, Sheba and Bob would share the Master bedroom, Donna would have her bedroom and there would be a guest bedroom. The remaining bedroom would be Sheba's sewing room. Bob was converting the huge finished basement into a workshop.

They'd behaved like three kids and had fun all day. But that was yesterday.

Now she stood at a distance, watching Bob leave her office. Finally, he decided to leave. She went in and got her jacket and bag, then hurried home before he could find her. Donna was home when she arrived and immediately knew something was wrong.

"What's the matter, Ma?"

Sheba held back her tears, but her voice was shaking as she told Donna what happened.

"Those dirty rats. You ought to get a transfer out of that place, Ma. Those people are crazy. Bob must be crazy too. How could he go with that old crow?"

"She's not so old. In fact, she's younger than I am."

"Well, she looks older than you do."

"Donna, she's only 31 years old and she looks darned good for her age."

"Yeah, but she looks so young because she clips rubber bands to her ears and ties them behind her head. Then she combs her hair to cover the rubber bands."

Sheba started laughing.

Donna, seeing she was cheering her mother up, continued.

"And when she laughs, she has to hold her lips together and let the sound come through her clenched teeth, so that her face won't wrinkle."

She gave her mother an example of what Pearl looked like while laughing. Donna contorted her face horribly. Sheba was laughing semi-hysterically.

"Can you imagine?" Donna went on, "Supposing the rubber bands burst?" She distorted her face to one side to show what she meant.

"Ma, that could be terribly embarrassing. Especially if it happened while she was talking to somebody, such as Bob, for instance."

They were both laughing when the phone rang. They looked at each other abruptly. Donna answered the phone.

"It's Bob, Ma."

"Tell him I can't talk to him right now,"

Donna gave Bob the message.

"He wants to know what time he can talk to you."

"Tell him I'll see him tomorrow morning at the office."

"He said if you don't come to the phone, he's coming over here right now."

Sheba went to the phone, reluctantly.

"Hello?" She could hardly speak above a whisper. Her voice suddenly became all choked up and she thought she would burst into tears all over again if she had to speak any louder.

"Sheba, darling, what is wrong?" He sounded very worried.

"Don't you know?"

"No, I don't. Are you feeling all right?"

"Yes, Bob. I'm all right."

"Is it something I've done to upset you or maybe something I haven't done?"

"Bob, please, I don't want to discuss it now. I'll see you tomorrow morning."

"I'm coming over, now."

"Please Bob, I'm begging you to wait."

She sounded so pitiful that he relented.

"All right, but I won't be able to sleep tonight."

"I'll see you tomorrow, Bob."

"Bye, sweetheart. Take good care of yourself."

Wearily, Sheba thought, "Into each life some rain must fall, but too much has fallen in mine."

She wondered where she heard those words before. Some blues song, she guessed, and some poor soul was in misery when they wrote the words. She didn't look forward to seeing him the next day.

Donna fixed some sandwiches for dinner and they both went to bed early.

The next morning, Sheba couldn't bring herself to get out of bed to go to work. The thought of seeing Bob terrified her. She and Donna stayed home.

When Sheba did not show up for work, Bob called her. Neither she or Donna answered the phone. Bob tried all day to reach her. His frustration made him unapproachable.

He closed his office door and told his secretary not to disturb him unless it was an emergency. All matters were to be taken care of by the Office Manager.

Several times he started to check out for the day and go to her house, intending to lean on her doorbell until she answered.

He was determined to find out what was wrong. It wasn't like her to keep things to herself, she was usually quite outspoken.

Late in the afternoon, Rachel asked if she could speak to him. She told him it was an emergency.

"May I speak with you, Mr. Dunn?" For the first time in her life, Rachel sounded timid She wanted to help this man. He was the first really decent man she'd ever met and did not deserve what had happened to him yesterday. Her conscience had whipped her all night and today. She decided to tell him the truth.

He looked awful to her, unshaven, wearing a wrinkled shirt. Usually, he was so clean that you could smell his soap all day long. Now his eyes even had bags under them, he probably hadn't slept a wink the previous night.

Bob wasn't in the mood to listen to anyone else's problems, but he clenched his teeth and nodded his head.

Rachel told Bob about the conversation between Pearl and Patricia.

"Would you tell that to Sheba?" He was relieved, he knew Sheba would believe him. "She isn't here today, but I will be indebted to you if you gave her all the facts. I didn't even know what made Sheba turn away. Thank you for coming in to me and explaining the situation."

As soon as Rachel walked out of his office, Bob walked out and drove straight to Sheba's apartment building.

He rang the doorbell and when someone looked through the peephole, he said, "Please let me in or I'll stand here all night ringing this bell."

A few minutes went by and he rang the bell again. Donna opened the door and let him into the apartment. She was clearly upset with him.

"My mother will be out in a few minutes." Then she disappeared into another room.

Bob stood in the middle of the living room floor. For the first time in Sheba's apartment, he felt unwanted and awkward.

When Sheba came out, she looked tense and worn to him. He knew that she didn't sleep either.

"Hello, Bob."

"Sheba, darling," he reached out for her, but she withdrew from his touch.

He dropped his arms to his sides. My GOD he thought, "she won't give me a chance.

Her hurt must be very deep."

"Sheba, I know how you must be hurting, I am too. I need you so much that I am breaking up inside. I just found out this afternoon what happened. Rachel came to my office and told me that she was in the lunch room when Pearl and Patricia made plans to break us up. I know how it must have looked to you, especially with Patricia telling you lies. Rachel also told me about that back room and what goes on there, I'm going to lay down some new laws about that."

"Bob, I'm sorry. I should have known better. I pride myself on being a free thinker and here I let Pearl, of all people, manipulate my thoughts, I could kick myself. She's like a man-eating shark."

He put his arms around her and held her close for a long time. When they kissed eagerly, both of them began to tremble and Sheba's knees almost crumpled under her.

"Bob, please let me sit down. I guess I've just gotten too emotionally involved with you."

"In other words, you love me too much, is that it?'

"Yes."

"Let's not wait, we can get married this weekend."

"We haven't finished the house yet."

"We'll finish it later."

"Bob, can you get me a transfer out of County Bureau #105?"

"Where would you like to work?" He was a little disappointed that she did not want to stay there and work with him, but he knew that it was best that she work at another agency in view of the situation.

"Some where in the main office, out of the welfare center and not supervising staff" "All right. I'll send all recruitment flyers to you by interoffice mail. You'll probably see something you like. I'll be looking to transfer to another agency myself after you leave. But be warned, Sheba, the main office always sounds good, but it is not what it seems. There are many drawbacks, especially for Black staff. It's not impossible to advance, but because there are some misfits in top management, it is very difficult. Also, the competition is keen for the few good positions that are vacated, there's a large number of back stabbers and cutthroats. Staff there can be brutal when it comes to competing for those provisionally appointed positions in management."

"Are you telling me that it's worse than here?"

"Working conditions are better there. Depending on where you are assigned, it can be environmentally pleasant as long as you are not in competition for a promotion."

"I guess I'll have to take my chances, Bob. You survived the main office. Knowing what went down at County Bureau #105, I don't think I will ever again feel comfortable there.

I know that there are some very good people working there, but the few that aren't so good can be exasperating."

"For your information, Pearl and Patricia are being transferred to a location in the ghetto. I took care of that before I left work. They have a surprise waiting for them in the morning."

"The ghetto."

"Yes. I think that's as close to Siberia as I could send them."

They both laughed.

They made plans for a Sunday wedding, both taking the next day off to get blood tests and the license. Bob returned to work on Wednesday, but Sheba took annual leave to shop

for a trousseau.

Donna was more excited than Sheba, if that was possible. This man was perfect for her mother and Sheba was perfect for him. It would have been worse than a crime if Pearl had succeeded in breaking them up.

The wedding took place at the local church after the last morning service. They were lucky to get the Reverend on such short notice, but Bob's parents were faithful and generous parishioners and they were obliged.

His mother and father were so happy, they cried. Bob was their only child. They had flown in from Texas just to be there for the wedding.

Donna was Sheba's maid of honor, Sheba's cousin, Charles, gave her away, Bob's best friend, Bernard, was best man. A friend of Bernard's was a photographer and took pictures of the wedding day.

Bob looked immaculately handsome in his Black custom-made tuxedo that he had from a previous occasion, while Sheba was exquisite in a light blue bouffant style gown of lace. Donna's short lace gown was baby pink and blended beautifully with her mother's outfit.

Everything was right, Sheba's Aunt Hetty whispered to her, "You'd better keep this man, there ain't very many men out there like that to be found," referring to Sheba's ex-husband.

Donna flew to Texas with Sheba, Bob and his parents. While Donna learned how to ride a horse, Bob and Sheba enjoyed a brief honeymoon on the ranch.

The three of them returned to New York the following Tuesday. While Sheba took a little more time off work, Donna returned to school, and Bob went back to work.

Not too long after that, a recruitment flyer came through for a job in the main office, in a section that was fairly new called the Bureau of Communications and Systems (BCS). They needed people with her title to be field representatives and to train staff on new procedures and policies.

Sheba felt she was capable of doing the job, according to the qualifications specified in the flyer, so she sent a brief resume. She really didn't expect an answer. To her surprise, she received a memo from Mrs. Ethel Green, who set up an appointment for Sheba.

Sheba's appointment was for 10a.m. the up coming Thursday. She decided she would not fuss for the interview, and wore pants, blouse and a big loose cowl-necked sweater because of the weather. Her leather boots matched her black pants and had a low heel for comfort.

She arrived a few minutes early, and was made to wait by the secretary's desk for twenty minutes as punishment.

Finally, she was shown into Mrs. Green's office.

Ethel Green sat at her desk, in a cramped office, so small that if Sheba stretched both arms could have touched the walls on either side of her. Sheba's office at County Bureau #105 was larger than Ethel Green's office.

Mrs.Green looked across the desk into Sheba's eyes, wondering whether or not Sheba would give her any competition with Steve. After a moment of reflection on this, she decided that she had no cause to worry in that area. Sheba was attractive, but too dark-skinned for Steve's taste. All of the women that Steve had been involved with that she knew about were interracial, one-night stands didn't count.

She smiled patronizingly at Sheba, very much like a White woman who was trying to convince a Black individual that she wasn't a racist.

"So! Tell me about yourself. Why do you want to leave County Bureau #105 and work for BCS?"

Sheba looked Ethel Green in the eye and stated firmly: "I want something new and more challenging, with better opportunities to advance."

"Bob Dunn is the director there? How do you like him?" Ethel asked slyly. She knew the rumor about Bob being engaged to this woman.

Sheba got the feeling that this woman had heard exactly what was happening at County Bureau #105. He had a few friends here in the main office.

"Bob is an excellent director and a wonderful man. None better. I could never say enough good things about him."

"Are you and he engaged?"

Ethel came right out with it, she was a little jealous and curious to know why Bob chose this woman. He had had many women chasing him when he worked in the main office, many beautiful women including herself. He was always polite, but he didn't mix with anybody at work until he got to County Bureau #105.

"No, we're married." Sheba said, deadpan."We were married a week ago."

"I didn't know the wedding would be so soon." Bob really was an excellent catch.

"We only invited our families." Sheba wanted to get back to business now. "Do you
have many field representatives now?"

"We have three and their supervisor."

"What centers would I cover?"

"The ones closest to your home, but occasionally, you may have to cover someone
else's center."

"What subject matter do you train?" Sheba asked.

"The work is quite diversified. It includes providing technical data processing assistance to the CRT staff and their supervisors, troubleshooting malfunctions in the computer systems by identifying equipment defects, auditing the welfare sites' systems and the staff's compliance with procedures to ensure effective operations. As a Training Specialist, I will also expect you to develop lesson plans and conduct training needs assessments for the new computer systems that are being installed. The Federal government will be installing a system of their own in a few years and you will be involved in that when the time comes. You have an excellent background for this work and it will be very challenging."

"What about advancement opportunities'"

"We expect this section to expand. It is one of the sections under Steve Beck, the Deputy Chief

Administrative Officer. As we expand, promotions will be given to those who deserve them."

If Sheba was as good as her performance evaluations said she was, she would be instrumental in helping Ethel to get Ralph Jensen' current director's job. Ethel was his assistant. She took more notes on Ralph's performance than she did on the staff that she supervised. Ralph Jensen was in deeper trouble than he realized.

Ethel looked expectantly at Sheba, "Do you have any more questions Mrs. Dunn?"

Sheba smiled at that. She wasn't quite used to her new surname.

"I can't think of any right now."

"Well then, thank you very much for coming to see me today. You will be hearing from me shortly." Ethel was smiling sincerely.

"Thank you for seeing me. I appreciate the opportunity." Sheba stood up to leave. "It was nice meeting you."

"My pleasure." Ethel returned. She had already made up her mind to hire her.

On the way back to County Bureau #105, Sheba tried to imagine life without County Bureau #105. It had to be better, in spite of all the negatives that Bob warned her about.

Sheba's thoughts drifted back to 1973 at Country Bureau #105, when the site was jammed with clients. There was no director at that time and Edith was the Office Manager. She was totally out of touch with all of her subordinates, usually in the supply room in a drunken stupor.

On one chaotic day, frontline staff needed all the support they could get from top management. What they got instead was unsympathetic and unintelligent orders from the people in the 'Ivory Tower' that caused an eruption of serious problems that could have led to tragedy. A woman strolled in at 12:30 pm, almost an hour late for her 11:30 am appointment. She argued with an interviewer that she should be seen immediately. The interviewer called Sheba. They both tried to explain to the woman that there were a lot of people ahead of her, people who had nine o'clock appointments. The woman argued with both of them heatedly. Not getting her own way, she became loud and ugly. Sheba called the patrolmen, they came and took the woman down to the patrol room.

The patrolmen took it upon themselves to call Edith, not realizing how drunk she was or the state of mind she was in, unfortunately.

They wanted someone to interview the woman right away and get her off their hands.

Edith didn't give a damn about anything at that moment, calling Sheba to order her to see the client right away.

Sheba let out a large sigh of disgust.

"Edith, it's not fair to the other clients. Some of them have been waiting here all morning with 9am appointments."

"Then send someone down to the patrol room to interview her. I want her out of here."

Sheba was very much annoyed as she walked over to Evelyn, who wasn't doing anything much as per usual. She was glad to go into the patrol room away from the unit. By the time Sheba got back to her desk, she could hear an uproar from the clients. She went back to the interviewers and found the clients getting out of control. No wonder. Evelyn was sitting at her desk interviewing the tardy client. The other clients resented the client who came in late being interviewed before them.

"Evelyn! I told you to do this in the patrol room."

"Don't take an attitude with me. The patrolmen sent her back upstairs, so I interviewed her here." Evelyn knew she was wrong but did not want to be reprimanded.

"Whatever happens now is your responsibility," Sheba went back to her desk.

But Sheba's troubles didn't end there. One of the male clients started a ruckus, stating "that the only way to get some service around here is to get loud and nasty."

When Sheba tried to talk to him, he got louder and nastier, then threatened her. She went to the phone to call the patrolmen and just as she picked up the phone, the man jumped over the barrier and walked menacingly towards her. When he got within five feet of her, she got a tight grip on the phone.

She gave him a deadly, fierce look, which stopped him dead in his tracks, and said in a clear, even voice, "Mister, before you do something stupid, you'd better remember that you bleed just like I do." The man glanced down at the phone in her hand and the way Sheba was holding it, then jumped back over the barrier to where he belonged.

He went back to his seat, next to a huge woman who looked like a professional male wrestler. The woman looked mean and tough. Sheba phoned for security. The woman shouted at her, "If them cops come up here and touch him, I am personally going to beat your Black ass myself. I will be waiting for you when you go home."

Although Sheba tried to put up a good front by steadily glaring at the big woman in a t-shirt, she was nervous about the situation. Many staff workers had been attacked by disgruntled clients. But this was the first time she had been threatened by a client who was the female version of King Kong.

Sheba did her best at all times to treat clients just as she would want to be treated if she were in a unfortunate situation. Most of the time when there was a problem, it was Pearl or Evelyn's lack of responsibility that caused it. Like the time the emaciated elderly woman came into the center with her landlord. Evelyn only budgeted the lady for food which was $47.00 dollars twice a month. Out of that, she was paying $37.50 each check for rent, which was $75.00 a month. When Sheba heard that, she nearly cried. The lady was starving.

Sheba made Evelyn issue as much back rent as the law allowed.

But, dealing with the woman in the t-shirt, Sheba just wanted to get through the afternoon with out having a breakdown. One of her co-workers, Florence, waited with her for the Office Manager, who promised to be there at five o'clock with a patrolman to see her to her car.

"It looks like Edith forgot about me, after starting all that trouble," Sheba said angrily.

"Yeah, what a mess. Say, look over there, isn't that the woman who threatened you? She's looking over here."

As Sheba looked at the woman, the look on the woman's face was pure fright. She ran into the patrol room. The woman, as tough as she looked, was afraid that Sheba and Florence were waiting to beat *her* up. The man with her had probably told the woman what Sheba said to him.

"I think we had better take this opportunity to split and go home. She'll be in there

for a few minutes."

Florence agreed. Without further ado, they made their way home safe and sound.

****

December 1979

Sheba started working at BCS in December of 1979. The very first test that Ethel put to Sheba, she came back with flying colors. Ethel, was ecstatic. Sheba proved to be an excellent trainer and writer. The thick lesson plans she submitted to Ethel were detailed and so was her method of training staff in the local sites.

The city was implementing a new Food Stamp form to be input by computer by the CRT operators at the local sites. The deadline for setting up and completing the training of all 120 sites was a day before the pending subway strike in January, 1980. Sheba had less than two weeks to schedule and notify more than 70 local welfare centers and other sites that had to be trained. There were over a thousand CRT operators, supervisors, all administrative and managerial staff involved. Sheba completed her assignment three days before the deadline. All of the CRT operators were ready and working on the new form when the strike began.

The rewards for bringing the project through on time gave Ethel and Steve Beck promotions. Sheba got nothing more than a pat on the head, but Ralph Jensen, as expected, lost his job to Ethel. She took all of the glory along with Steve.

Sheba thought about what she'd heard about the 'glass ceiling'. It was for people uniquely different from the traditional upper management, such as Black women and other minority groups. Rarely did minorities 'break through the glass ceiling'. They could look up and see top management, but they were not allowed there.

In spite of this, when Ethel continued to give Sheba complicated training projects, Sheba continued to come through for her. Ethel continued to get promotions, and raises and Sheba continued to get nothing. No breaking through that 'glass ceiling' for her.

Training became big at BCS. It expanded so much that Steve obtained larger office space for the department. Ethel gave Sheba the grand title of "Training Coordinator" and allowed her to share an office with the supervisor, Theodore Steiner, but still there was no promotion.

Finally, after Sheba proved she could handle her assignments and had created over 100 training sessions, Ethel broke down and gave her a merit increase because Theodore pressured her to do something positive. Ethel never let Sheba forget what she did for her.

As a result of Sheba's receiving the merit increase and a new title, a few of the other field workers began to resent her and called her 'Ethel's Pet'. They formed a clique and as new field workers were recruited they would tell them to "watch out for Sheba, she's in Ethel's good graces."

They were afraid that Sheba would move up and leave them behind, so they did everything they could to undermine her in Ethel's eyes.

One of the leaders in the clique was a gay man, Kenny Franklin. He seemed to resent Sheba the most. He was already working when she started there and didn't want her to advance before he did.

Kenny Franklin had no civil service status. He was hired by Steve Beck in the clerical title of Office Associate, three levels below Sheba's civil service title of Principle Administrative Associate. Most of the clique had civil service job status, but their titles were also below Sheba's.

Steve met Kenny on the streets of Mega City. Steve was on his lunch hour and had to run over to the Federal Building on Main Street.

It was just beginning to rain lightly and Kenny was thinking of calling it a day, when Steve Beck saw him, on the street, singing his heart out. As Steve stopped to watch and listen to Kenny, he thought that although the man wasn't really talented, he was good to look at. When Kenny finished singing, people threw coins at him. Steve took out his wallet and handed him ten dollars and a business card. All Steve said was, "Call me anytime."

Kenny's eyes widened at the denomination of the bill and answered "Any special time?"

Steve smiled at him. "I'm usually there between 7 A.M. and 7 P.M. If I'm not there, leave a message with my secretary, a number where I can reach you." Kenny made a note on the back of Steve's business card. They shook hands and Steve left.

Kenny contacted Steve the next day at 7:30 A.M.. Steve told him he could get him a job and made an appointment to see him that afternoon. Kenny showed up wearing his very best audition suit, a dark brown double-breasted model, with matching shoes, at 3 P.M. sharp. Steve informed his secretary that he did not want to be disturbed.

By the time the interview was over, Kenny had both a job and a lover.

Kenny smiled triumphantly to himself as he rode down in the main office's elevator.

He couldn't wait to tell Timmie about his day.

When he arrived home, Timmie wasn't there. Kenny walked straight into the bedroom and studied himself in the full-length mirror. He gazed lovingly at his own reflection, smiling at himself. Pleased with that smile, he tried several others. First, a broad smile, showing all of his teeth. Then, he smiled with his lips together, no teeth showing, Varying the intensity and the length of his smiles, he decided he looked good, no matter how he smiled. Whether he was on the streets singing for money or being interviewed for a job or meeting a lover, he always wanted to look good. That would get him the big bucks.

He removed his clothes slowly, and got carried away with a sensual exhilaration, just as his live-in lover walked in and advanced toward him with a leer.

Kenny was not a native from Mega City. His hometown was Miami, Florida, and occasionally he would visit his family there. Glenda Bush, a co-worker at BCS, would go with him on these visits, both pretending to be full-time lovers. It wasn't a total lie, as Glenda was very kinky and into hard-core porn. Sometimes she would let Kenny do weird things to her. Kenny was pretty pleased with himself whenever he could perform with a woman, no matter how kinky. Glenda labeled herself as bi-sexual, and belonged to the clique that wanted to get Sheba out of BCS.

They were out to exact their pound of flesh from Sheba, each in his or her own way.

Kenny waited for a day when Theodore Steiner was absent for the day, then strolled into the office Sheba shared with Theodore. He made himself comfortable at Theodore's desk and proceeded to use the telephone. When it became clear that Kenny was talking to a fellow homosexual, Sheba wondered why he choose *her* for a captive audience. The conversation on Kenny's end was obscene and ludicrous. She left the office to go the ladies' room, to give him time to complete the call and return to his own desk, which held a working telephone.

Sheba stayed as long as she could stand it. As disgusting as the ladies' room was, still

it was better than the filth Kenny was spouting, but she eventually had to return to her desk. She at least, had work to do and deadlines to meet.

When she arrived back in the office, her heart fell. He was still there. The man went on and on, bringing to Sheba's mind a shot on TV of a large mouth running incessantly, a motor mouth. An obscene motor mouth.

She gathered up work to take to the copier, knowing that if she approached him, it would start a major controversy. The clique would back him up, no matter what he did. If one got mad at you, they all got mad at you, unjust or not.

At least she got one break, the copier machine was working. Robin was there making copies and had quite a few to make. Sheba was glad, she liked Robin, she was a very pleasant woman and a joy to talk with. She parked herself on some boxes and waited. It was a half hour before she got the machine, but she and Robin had some decent conversation. Shortly after Sheba got the copier machine, Kenny walked out of the office, apparently disappointed because he was devoid of an audience. He had a strong, foul body odor and, as he walked by, he left some of it behind. It reminded Sheba of a dead rat.

****

1984

Mildred Cantor, one of Sheba's co-workers at BCS, sat at her desk, brooding over her last encounter with Ethel. The woman had accused Mildred of being incompetent and unable to handle her job. Mildred was officially a field worker, but was really in the office all the time. Ethel told her that she had better start looking for an Income-Maintenance center or Food Stamp site that she preferred working in, or she would be transferred to one involuntarily.

At first, Mildred could not believe her ears. Here was this Black woman, one who seemed to wish she was White, threatening her, a White woman, with the equivalence of exile.

The local sites were considered battlegrounds, a source of stress and high blood pressure for most of the staff that worked there. Upset clients not only threatened the workers, but a few were desperate and dangerous enough to take violent action against staff that did not hand over a check on demand. Sometimes it was because a client did not or refused to comply with departmental procedures. Recent prison releasees would sometimes threaten the staff, claiming they did not mind going back to prison if they did not get what they want. What they meant was, "Give me a check or else."

Sometimes it worked, depending on the worker. There were workers as tough as the clients, who carried knives and guns in holsters around their ankles. Even the supervisors kept lead pipes and mace in their desk drawers, ready to use to ward off any impending danger. Clients were known to leap over the gates and charge at workers like raging bulls. At the risk of losing their jobs, instead of their lives, workers defended themselves as best they could.

Most of the time, the workers would let the clients have what they were entitled to, without any fuss. But certain benefits needed higher approval, and if the worker had an unreasonably nasty supervisor, watch out. That type of supervisor would reject the request just because the worker did not cross her T's. The workers soon learned that by giving the clients the offending boss' name and location, they could get the approval they needed. Why should the workers take all the flack?

Mildred considered all of these things and did not wish to return to the centers. The word was that just last week a disturbed client had walked into a center, singled out a worker, and sliced her up before the patrolmen could stop her. The worker lived, but was too disabled, mentally and physically to ever work again. She retired on disability at a very young age.

Tears welled up in Mildred's eyes. Although she was White and had a college degree, she was 60 years old. Her hair was all gray and she weighed over two hundred fifty pounds. No way she could get the promotion she wanted in a local site Upper management positions were limited, and given to friends of management.

She brooded all week, finally deciding to write an anonymous letter to Ethel and tell her off. Not thinking that it might have dire consequences for the rest of the staff. Early Thursday morning before any of the other staff arrived, she sat at Moreaver's (Ethel's secretary) typewriter and copied the notes she had created at home. Every grievance and complaint she could think of, both personal and business, went into that letter. Not once did she get specific about her own problems, knowing that Ethel would then identify the author of the cowardly missive.

Mildred was quite skilled at typing, it had been her first job into Civil Service. The unsigned letter was finished in a few minutes. She hurried to lay it in plain view on Ethel's desk so that Ethel would see it the moment she sat down.

Somehow, Mildred managed to contain herself until Ethel came to work. She hoped that Ethel would throw a tantrum or do something equally stupid, but she was sorely disappointed. Ethel maintained her cool, outwardly at least, and questioned staff about its origin. Of course, nobody knew anything.

At least, Mildred thought, I'll give her stupid ass something to think about. She'll be wondering for the rest of her life who hated her enough to write that letter. Mildred believed she was the avenging angel for Ralph Jensen, the former director, as well as herself. Ethel tried to pretend she was such a humanitarian when it came to her staff, but she deliberately brutalized the people with whom she worked. Everything she did not want to happen to her, she inflicted upon others.

Not long after, Mildred announced her retirement. Ethel was there, smiling at the big party and luncheon staff threw for Mildred. In fact, Ethel made the most moving speech given there.

Ethel stared blindly at the letter in her hands, with rage burning in her eyes and face. A hot flush of hate and humiliation covered her like an electric blanket charged to maximum heat.

Someone had put an anonymous letter on her desk, and it was one of her staff members.

She knew that some of them resented her, but the person who wrote this harbored such a deep loathing and hatred for her that the letter made her feel very uncomfortable and very unsafe.

With not the slightest idea or clue of who the guilty party was, she decided that she was intelligent enough to figure out the perpetrator. Yes, in her mind, this was a crime against her.

Hadn't her mother, who was a White woman, taught her that she was better that most people? She told her that her mixed blood, the blood of an Irish woman and the blood of a thoroughbred Black man, gave her an advantage over both races. In fact, this blood gave her superiority over any race in the world.

She thought of each staff member, in turn, and immediately rejected the thought that any of the White men could have written such a letter to her. The very thought was abhorrent and sent a cold chill up her spine. Every lover she ever had was White and she knew she had many White admirers just about every White male who looked at her.

Secretly, she considered herself White, even though her father and paternal grandmother were Black. Ethel worshipped her mother, she could do no wrong. Therefore, all White people could do no wrong.

As she went over the remaining staff members in her mind, men of all colors were eliminated, as she tossed her waist-length, wavy, coal-black hair. It was a woman, it had to be, they were all very jealous of her. Why shouldn't they be? She was beautiful and intelligent, and every man who laid eyes on her, wanted her, except Sheba's husband, Bob. A flash of jealousy shot through her. She had really wanted the man. At first, when she flirted with him, while he worked at the main office, he showed a flicker of interest. After he found out she was married, he was polite and platonic only. When Steve moved up in status, he made a move on her, so she accepted his offer to move up with him. But Ethel was still disappointed when Bob got a promotion and left to go the local welfare center.

Now, Sheba had Bob, and from what Ethel heard and saw, they were both monogamous. Steve had expressed an interest in Sheba, but she ignored his hints and the fact that he tried to sit by her at every meeting. Ethel pretended that she didn't notice what he was doing, but it was the same approach Steve had used on her.

Her eyes narrowed as she continued to contemplate the letter in front of her. Which one of those Black bitches did this to her.

"They're all to stupid," she thought, carefully going over every word, "Except Sheba." The letter was well-written and highly intelligent and in her closed mind, only Sheba of the entire BCS staff, could write that well.

Reaching for her buzzer to summon Moreaver, her secretary, Ethel started forming a plan for revenge in her mind. Sheba would pay dearly for this.

When Moreaver walked in, Ethel stared at her for a few minutes, the letter was typewritten. Maybe Moreaver did it? No, the woman was too stupid. Unless, of course, she typed it for Sheba. Now that was a distinct possibility.

"You buzzed me, Ethel?"

The woman was stupid. Who else in hell could have buzzed her? Ethel handed her the letter and watched her reaction.

"Who put this on my desk?" Ethel's voice was cold and hard.

Moreaver read the letter slowly and fright was beginning to overtake her. Ethel probably thought *she* wrote that nasty letter.

"I don't know Ethel. They musta' done it after I went home yesterday."

Ethel frowned. That let Sheba out as she went home the same time as Moreaver. Wait a minute, Sheba always got in very early.

"What time does Sheba get in the office?"

"Why? Do you think she did this?" Moreaver asked, dumbfounded. She couldn't wait to gossip.

"I don't want you to discuss this with anybody. Tell the entire staff I am going to hold a meeting tomorrow morning at ten o'clock in my office. Make enough copies of that letter for everyone."

The new office was large enough to accomodate a long conference table, suitable for seating ten individuals. Ethel was plotting her strategy. Sheba would be sorry she wrote that letter for the rest of her life. She would make sure that Sheba never got another promotion or a transfer to a requested office.

Meanwhile the author of the anonymous letter waited nervously for all hell to break loose. Mildred pretended to be hard at work writing memos for distribution. Although her memos were always well-written as a result of her long years in service and faithful attendance at college, Ethel never acknowledged that Mildred ever did anything well. She was too fat. The bad feelings were mutual between each other and got worse when Ethel sabotaged Ralph

Jensen out of his job. Mildred had been devoted to him.

Just before Mildred departed from BCS, she informed Sheba about Ethel's climb up.

"But, of course, Ethel isn't the first to wheel-and deal for a promotion. Whether the job is in government or private industry, that's standard practice. It just seems worse in government because there isn't supposed to be discrimination of any kind. Talent, ability to perform in a position, as well as the city's written examinations, are supposedly the prime factors in selecting employees." Mildred's bitterness showed up in her voice. The procedures and policies of BCS and DPO (Data Processing Office) have nothing to do with mandated government law. The primary factors in job appointment or promotions, in this particular section, according to the unwritten law, are erotic sex, drugs, treachery, deceit, sadism, brutality, racism, dangerous indifference to sexually transmitted diseases, unjust vengance against the innocent, favoritism, backstabbing cutthroats, vicious gossips, psychotics, managerial stupidity and pettiness, greed and the obsessive desire to do anything to get ahead. I guess I've covered everything except murder, but I wouldn't be surprised if they haven't already tried that. What they do in the meantime, what they do now, is tantamount to murder. They play games with people's livelihood and get away with it."

Sheba gave thought to what she'd said to her long after Mildred retired. She was to find out for herself the truth in her words. Maybe Mildred was right in saying it's an impossible task to get a promotion if you don't give in to 'politicking'. So be it, she would resign herself to staying at this level until she retired.

Ethel had no intention of ever giving Sheba a promotion if she could help it. The anonymous letter, in addition to Steve's fascination with Sheba ensured that. Bob Dunn, Sheba's husband, was coming back to the main office to take over a new section, Welfare Federated Systems (WFS). He was going to be in the same building with BCS.

So, when an opening came up in Ethel's group for a Deputy Director, Ethel refused to select one of her current staff. Theodore Steiner, capable of doing the job with good rapport with his subordinates, was overlooked. He was very angry when Ethel chose to bring in an outsider and he started submitting resumes to other agencies. One of his friends in DPO needed an assistant and Theodore was transferred there, gaining a well-deserved promotion.

The person Ethel selected for the Deputy Director's job sent chills up Sheba's spine. It was Agatha Fluddrucker, the ex-director of County Bureau #105 who was caught with Paul McDonald. She was just as nasty as ever, hadn't learned a thing in all those years and still could not relate to staff. Agatha managed to make the staff hate Ethel even more. She started undermining Ethel the moment she arrived in BCS.

When Bob got his new unit, Sheba transferred there on a loan basis. Ethel did not want Sheba completely out of her control. She wanted to be able to prevent Sheba from advancing.

Meanwhile, Ethel decided that Moreaver needed help with the typing and took on a public assistance recipient as her assistant.

The assistant typist was Emmaline Spenser, a sad-eyed Black woman with goldenbrown skin and long, thick, wavy hair. The County was using her welfare checks as her salary, and told her if she performed well on the job she would be recommened for a full-time, well paying, provisional position with the County.

Agatha began to take over a lot of Ethel's chores because the new computer system, WFS, was being installed by the Federal government even though the jobs were being manned by County and State employees. There were many complex subsystems and technologies to be learned, and Ethel was responsible for learning all of them. She had to attend scores of meetings. At the same time, Ethel wanted out of BCS, not only was the staff making her life miserable, she also wanted to make more money. She and her husband bought a house in a very exclusive section of Mega City. Fortunately for her, Steve had become the Commissioner's Deputy Assistant and gave Ethel a substantial promotion to a job title nobody had ever heard of before.

After Ethel left, Agatha became the director of BCS. She was less liked by every one at BCS than Ethel. Agatha was down right mean. The only person she managed to get along with was Emmaline. Agatha took Emmaline under her wing and helped her to make fast progress on the job. The rumors began to fly about Agatha and Emmaline.

Before Sheba went over to WFS, she would occasionally have talks with Emmaline. The same clique that gave Sheba a hard time was now concentrating on Emmaline. Sheba no longer posed any threat to them, although they didn't like her any better. Her husband Bob, dropped by the office the day he was being interviewed by the Commissioner for the position as head of WFS. The eyeballs were rolling with jealousy at Sheba. Bob was the best-looking man they'd ever seen and there he was, being attentive and loving to Sheba of all people. While he was in Sheba's office, every woman on the floor found an excuse to visit Sheba's office, including Agatha.

After that day, Emmaline used Sheba as a sounding board and to get sympathy. She would tell Sheba how much everybody at BCS hated her except Sheba, and that they said terrible things to her and about her. By the time Emmaline finished talking with her, Sheba felt very sorry for the woman. She was pitiful and pitable. Emmaline's self-esteem was zilch. Even she was continually saying bad things about herself. Sheba would speak to Agatha for Emmaline whenever she saw her in an approachable mood. Eventually talked her into giving her two promotions on a provisional basis.

Underneath that 'pitiful' exterior, Emmaline was really quite hardboiled. She was what street people call 'Two-Faced'. She would pretend to Sheba that she hated Agatha and in turn would go back to Agatha with every word that Sheba spoke, without missing a vowel or a consonant. She played a dangerous game, being used to a tough street life and untold misery and suffering. In her game, she wanted to be the focus of both Agatha's and Sheba's attention.

The reality was that Emmaline craved to inevitably mean more, to both of them than their families. The more she realized that this would never be, the more dangerous and thwarted she became, leading to her own tragic demise.

Hating the staff of BCS with an unfounded passion, she did everything in her power to hurt them as they hurt her.

Emmaline knew that Agatha and Sheba would protect her from them as much as they could.Sheba helped her because she felt very sorry for her. Emmaline had pored her heart and soul out to her, about her miserable past, which was even worse than her present life. Agatha helped her because she was using and abusing Emmaline, the latter submitting out of desperation to keep her job.

So, never having been truly loved before in her life, Emmaline felt arrogant with her power. The Christmas party was coming up. She was delighted when Agatha paid thirty dollars for her ticket. Having heard about previous parties, she was duty-bound to bring her camera there.

The evening of the Christmas party, after work, Agatha brought her to the fabulous Red Apple Restaurant and Bar.

Once there and ensconced at a table, Agatha and Emmaline went their separate ways.

Emmaline prowled the Christmas party at the Red Apple, with her instant camera. She maliciously made it a point to snap her co-workers at their very worst. These were the people who made her life miserable on a daily basis at BCS. Some got drunk beyond consciousness, while others were intoxicated and behaving badly.

Ethel Green couldn't keep her hands off Steve Beck, and snuggled up to him intimately while dancing. His wife sat at a table, glowering jealously at them. When a fast tune with a steady beat came on, Steve gave up and went over to a group of men to talk. Ethel stayed on the floor and all the men turned to watch her. They knew would happen next. It happened every year at every Christmas party.

In a tight-fitting red dress, Ethel moved to the beat of the upbeat rhythm with a sensous boogey. The more she bent her knees, the higher her dress crept, until all of her thighs were on display. She twisted her way to the center of the floor. Losing all of her inhibition, with the help of straight scotch whiskey, Ethel tossed her long thick hair in every direction. She kicked her legs up as high as they could go, displaying red underwear to match her red dress. Most people there would have bet a week's salary that she wasn't wearing anything at all under the dress. Steve came over and stopped her. After all, she was in a critical postion at the office and needed to be taken seriously.

When Ethel sat down, Gertude Hardwick got on the floor and was determined to "outdance" Ethel. With her gray hair and long skinny legs flying, she took her flared dress by the hem and flung it, so that the men would not miss anything. They didn't. Kenny leaned over and whispered to Ilene.

"She needs to take her gray ass and sit down. Granny needs a rocking chair, not a shake dance. She's just making a fool of herself."

"What about Ethel?" Ilene said jealously.

"Ethel is one good-looking, sexy woman." Kenny answered with a lustful grin. He was remembering the time the three of them, Ethel, Steve and himself were in bed together. Ethel performed like a polished prostitute and the evening was a smashing success. Steve had some cocaine there and it made everything smoother.

Meanwhile, Emmaline, still scouting around with her camera, had taken several pictures of Ethel and Gertrude. She was now trying to get pictures of Ilene, in her skin-tight pink jumpsuit. Circling around in back of Ilene and Kenny, she got a good shot of Ilene's rear end. Neither of them noticed the flash.

Camera in hand and ready for some real action, she passed a darkened stairwell. Peering through the dark there, she had almost missed Jewel Brooks and Mark Goldberg, kissing passionately. His tongue was deep in her mouth. Focusing in on them, Emmaline pulled the lever. The bright light stunned and frightened them. They were both married to other people. Their spouses did not take kindly to extra-marital affairs. Mark, on occasion, wore a Yarmulka to profess his religious status. Jewel, on the other hand, was married to a truck driver who looked like a Black version of the Incredible Hulk. As Emmaline walked away, the couple darted up the stairs after her.

"Emmaline!" Jewel called sharply.

Emmaline stopped a few feet away and turned to look at her watch with a insolent look on her face, which drained the fight out of Jewel.

"Emmaline," Jewel's voice was meek now. "I'll give you five dollars for that picture."

Emmaline thought for a moment. That wasn't bad, considering she paid that amount for a whole package of film. To sell it, though, meant spoiling her fun in the future to tease Jewel. She examined the instant picture and laughed. Humiliated, Jewel got the five dollars from Mark and handed it to Emmaline. Both looked relieved when she gave them the picture.

From that day forward, Jewel hated Emmaline with a passion.

Emmaline went back to the table to see how Agatha was faring. Agatha was standing with Ethel and Clovis Flambud, Ethel's immediate supervisor. The outfit that Agatha had on was bizarre.

She had come into Emmaline's cubicle wearing a micro-mini, slinky black leatherdress, so low cut that her nipples kept threatening to make a full, personal appearance. It was so short it embarrassed Emmaline to look at it. Agatha had arrived at work at eight that morning, wanting Emmaline to tell her how she looked.

She said if Emmaline had disapproved, she would have gone home and changed her clothes.

Moreaver had come into work before Emmaline, but Agatha waited until Emmaline came in before modeling that dress. Turning around and posing, waiting for Emmaline's reaction to her clothes.

Emmaline was so shocked, she just stood with her mouth open. This is the woman who criticized Sheba for wearing a dress one-quarter of an inch, above her knees. Agatha was wearing ankle-length dresses at the time.

Agatha mistook Emmaline's horror for approval and said, "I see you approve."

Knowing better than to disagree with Agatha, Emmaline replied, "Agatha, it's unbelieveable. I'm speechless." She wasn't lying, she was speechless and did not know what to say to her. Emmaline thought Agatha looked like a penny whore.

The outfit was tailormade for Agatha, every bone in her body was visible in the too tight dress. Thinking she had Emmaline's approval, she marched around all day in the outfit. The entire staff gossiped all day about the director's dress.

Moreaver, who was now Agatha's secretary since Ethel refused to take her with her to the new job, remarked, "Agatha should be ashamed of herself. She should have worn office clothes to work and changed to that outfit after work."

The party wasn't until 7pm.

The day after the party, none of the top management staff showed up for work, including Agatha. Emmaline had taken a taxi home from the party when she saw that Agatha would not be able to drive.

Gertude Hardwick came in the following day, bragging about what a fine time she had had at the Christmas party. She had worn a see-through dress with no slip underneath, thinking she looked beautiful, cool and seductive. Her short gray hair had been combed in the usual style, brushed straight back with no curl. She had a sallow complexion with scores of wrinkles, which she claimed she was proud of along with her long, boney arms and legs.

Once the music started, she did not sit down or stop drinking. Doing the Limbo and other tropical dances, she was so drunk, she started pulling up her dress and showing off *her* red underwear. Gertrude treated every man there to a look at her entire leg and thigh.

The staff couldn't stop talking about her, calling her "Granny" behind her back, and saying she carried on worse than a teenager. These were her friends talking about her, members of the clique.

One of them said facetiously to her face, "Oh, you had a nice time last night."

Gertrude replied, "That 's what I went there for, I paid my money to be there."

When Eileen McMurray came back from the Data Processing Office, she said to Gertrude, "Gertie, I heard about you all the way to DPO. What did you do at the party?"

Gertrude replied coolly," I just had a nice time."

Eileen said, "Oh yeah? People were saying you really danced."

Gertrude smiled. She felt very triumphant, she'd shown up Ethel. Everybody loved the way she danced better, and she was a few years older than Ethel.

Eileen remembered that her friend Gertrude flirted with young men less that half her age, bouncing around them like a teenager. Rumor had it she was having an affair with Laird Cosby, married and 22 years old. The rumor also said that she bought his daily supply of coke.

It was ludicrous because Gertrude looked, in Eileen's opinion, as if she were at least 70 years old and too dried up to have an affair with anybody, including her steady boyfriend, whom she called "Mr. Bryant". He looked about 80 years old himself.

When Agatha came in, she bragged to Emmaline that Clovis had to drive her home, she was so drunk. Agatha said she fell asleep in the back seat of Clovis' car. By the time they arrived at Agatha's house in Lincolnvale, her husband had to come outside and carry her inside to bed.

AGENCY PROCEDURES; LUST and CORRUPTION

****

<u>1985</u>

Marish Maquid

Marish Maquid Zabed sat at the CRT terminal. This would be his permanent assignment while he stayed in Mega City. He hoped it would be interesting, at least as far as women were concerned. So far, he had not seen anyone who caught his fancy. Most of the staff were temporarily at the local sites, but would be back to the WFS office soon. His partner, Gerard Marx, was an older man on the State payroll, while Marish worked for a private company, SDE.

When Bob, Sheba's husband walked in and said, "Hello." Marish glanced up at him and returned his greeting. Bob sat down at one of the terminals, which he rarely did, and began to input some data. Marish turned back to his own terminal.

A telephone rang in the distance, then a few seconds later a soft voice called "Bob, telephone." Marish looked up into the eye of the most striking woman he'd ever met. Her features were African and soft. The red loose blouse she wore enhanced her warm, dark brown skin. He could feel his mouth covering her mouth and immediately felt the sensation in his libido. Incredible! Marish had once worked for the Playboy club and met many sensuous beauties, but none had this strong and wonderful sensation of pure and unadulterated animal magnetism.

Marish was impatient to get to know her, feeling sure that all this woman had to do was look at him and she would be his for the asking.

From that moment on, Marish concentrated his efforts toward seducing Sheba. He was not aware that Sean Garrison, Sheba's supervisor had similar desires.

Staff meetings were held every Thursday morning at ten. When Bob and Sheba walked into the conference room together, although they were not holding hands, the electricity between them was obvious to everyone else in the room. Marish was already seated at the table next to Gerard, and both men stared at Sheba with jaws hanging. Marish was visibly shaken to his roots. She was all he had ever wanted in a woman.

Sheba and Bob said "Good morning," and seated themselves together at the table opposite Marish, but further toward the end. Marish had to turn in his seat to look at her, which he did all through the meeting, desperately trying to catch her eye. Sheba deliberately ignored him. It was easy, she had Bob.

Bob's chair was as close to Sheba's as it could get and Marish was boiling with jealousy. Every now and then, Bob's hand would brush Sheba's and an electric shock would go through both of them. He did this as often as he could, trying to avoid attracting too much attention from staff. Marish was aware of every touch.His eyes glowered and penetrated Sheba like a knife. She refused to look at him.

In the meantime, Bob's boss, Steve Beck, was also very much aware of Sheba's presence. He had wanted her for a long time, ever since they were Training Specialists together.Although he wasn't as obvious as Marish, his eyes would linger on Sheba as long as possible. He too, felt pangs of jealousy because of Sheba's closeness to her husband. Sometimes he wished that he and his wife had what Bob and Sheba had in their marriage.

Now, as Steve looked over at Sheba, she was in turn looking at Bob with such tenderness that it made his heart turn over. As he looked down at the papers in front of him, he was determined to have Sheba for himself. Married or not. Most of his women were married to other men. They were easier to handle that way. He could offer her more than Bob, monetarily. Steve glanced over at her again, and was amazed all over again at how young she looked. She was older than anybody there, except Gerard Marx, who was sixty-five and her husband, who was 5 years older than Sheba. Steve wondered how she managed to keep herself looking so good. She was now a grandmother, but it was almost impossible to believe to look at her.

The more he looked, the more he wanted, until he could imagine holding her in his arms and pressing his lips against hers. Sheba's lips were very inviting, her figure superb and he had never seen a more magnificent pair of legs on anybody. No wonder Bob was hooked.

Steve knew it wasn't going to be easy, but if Bob could get her, so could he. Although Bob was taller and far better-looking, Steve was sure his power and influence would get him what he wanted.

When the meeting was over, Bob and Sheba remained seated, gazing into each others eyes. Marish walked over to them and said, "I'm glad to see you here, Sheba.I missed you last week."

"Thank you, Marish. Bob and I flew to his parents' ranch in Texas. How are you? I've been meaning to ask you, how is your wife? Have you become a daddy yet?'

Marish blushed and said, "No, I haven't been back to Bombay yet." He stared at her a few seconds, then Gerard came over and kissed Sheba on the cheeks. Here was a man who really loved his beautiful oriental wife. His wife was into creative arts, and often gave shows of her works. Gerard said, "What took you so long? I thought I was going to retire before you came back from vacation." Sheba smiled and said. "I'm glad to see you, too. We took another honeymoon, for our tenth year of marriage."

Marish and Gerard chatted for a few minutes, then left. Steve walked over and took Sheba's hand and kissed it tenderly. Sheba was surprised, but kept her cool. Bob was annoyed. That was Steve's signal that he was going to try to compete for Sheba's affection. Steve was a very greedy man.

Bob sighed. He knew that he did not have to worry about Sheba, but his concern was that Steve might try to cause problems for him and or Sheba when he could not get his way. He wasn't about to give Sheba up to Steve or anybody else. Bob was aware of how Sheba's magnetism attracted men to her and was grateful that she choose him.There simply was nobody else like her.He knew he attracted many women, but until he met Sheba, he hadn't really known what love was.

Both Sheba and Bob's first marriages were luke-warm compared to the great intensity of heat that he and Sheba generated together. After ten years, it just got better and better, their love was like a perennially blossoming flower. When they went to church, he felt that GOD had made this marriage and he thanked GOD for blessing him with Sheba.

Bob was ready to retire from the City, he would be 55 in two years. They planned to to sell the house and move to Texas, His parents wanted them to take over the management of the ranch. He had already spoken to a real estate agent and was amazed at the fantastic amount of money the Island house would bring. The view of the ocean was magnificent and having a sizable portion of the beach didn't hurt either. At first, they offered Donna and her husband the house, but when those two separated and divorced, Donna and her four little children preferred to come live on the ranch with them.

After the meeting, Bob went into Sheba's office to eat his lunch. His wife had made tuna sandwiches today, it was raining and they didn't want to go out to eat. He went to the little refrigerator in her office, pulling out two sodas and some fresh fruit. Bob pulled his chair as close to Sheba's as he could and took one of the sandwich halves. Just as he started to sip his soda, there was a knock on the door. Sean came into the office, closing the door behind him.

Sean's eyes took in Bob's chair right next to Sheba's. A look of jealousy flashed across his face, but his voice was controlled.

"You're at lunch now, Sheba?" He asked.

"Yes, we just started. Is there something urgent to be taken care of?" Sheba and Bob hoped he could wait.

174

"That's okay, I'll see you afterward. That looks good." Sean was looking at the sandwiches.

"Have a sandwich. We can afford to share."

Sean reached out and took one of the halves. He glanced at Bob enviously, then took a huge bite out of the sandwich. Still chewing voraciously, he left.

Bob looked at Sheba tenderly and said, "He loves you."

Sheba didn't look at him as she replied, "I don't think so. He was probably just hungry."

"Yes, hungry for you."

Sheba laughed, "You love me, so naturally you think every man who looks at me is in love with me."

"I'm the only man who is in love with you, because you love me too. What I said is that Sean loves you without any reciprocal love from you."

Sean was a product of the Hippy revolution turned Yuppie. He was tall, good-looking and built like Superman, the movie version. His resemblance to Christopher Reeves was uncanny to say the least. He was born and bred in Oklahoma, but had a slight Texan drawl. Even with his business suits, he wore cowboy boots. Sean had a wife and three sons, all in college, supported by him and his wife's salary as a lawyer in the District Attorney's office.

His wife Priscilla knew full well of Sean's extra-marital affair with Clovis, but since she was having her own affair with her boss, she kept quiet. It was all in the game of upward mobility. No love involved, only sex.

Sean, on the other hand, had a conscience.He wasn't a blatant ladies' man but, because of his good looks, he'd had his share of women. His strong attraction to Sheba had him in a dilemma. The desire and heat burning inside him was getting stronger every day. He deluded himself that if he approached her,she would respond favorably. Never having been turned down by a woman, he was confident of his quarry. He had to make the first move, Sheba damn sure wasn't going to come to him. She was pleasant to him, but not flirtatious. Practically every woman in that section had made advances to him, but not Sheba.

Today, after the meeting, he was going to give her an opportunity to do so. If she did not, he would say something. Maybe that's what she was waiting for, he would make a joke of it and see what happened.

Sean went directly to his office and snorted some coke. Clovis kept him supplied. For fifteen minutes he sat there, getting spaced out, almost forgetting Sheba. When she came back into his thoughts, he headed for her office. The door was closed. So much the better they would be alone.

Taking a deep breath, he knocked on the door, then boldly walked in, not giving her a chance to answer. Bob was sitting there practically in her lap, eating lunch with her. Sean seethed inside with fury and jealousy. The strong emotions made the coke wear off quickly. He was in and out of there in less than a minute.

Marish also, was disappointed. He too. thought that his power over women was so strong that Sheba would have been his to toy with by nightfall. It was incredible that she preferred her husband over him.

Marish was having a kinky affair with a woman in Boston. She was white and married. Either he flew there or she would come to him. At one time, he had wanted desperately to marry her. He was lonely for love and the woman played upon this. Esther Ginsbar, Marish's lover, had a wealthy husband, but no money of her own. She couldn't afford to divorce her husband and marry Marish, whose income was barely above the poverty level. Her husband was a millionaire and allowed her wide latitude with his checkbook. She liked the luxurious style of living and was not about to forego it for Marish.

Esther's husband used her to promote his business affairs. She slept with his business friends when necessary and was hostess at all of his dinner parties.

Her husband Jake had a very young mistress, his secretary, who was being groomed to take his wife's place. Eventually Esther would be too old and would no longer be of use to him. She was beginning to show wear-and-tear from so much running around.

Esther was very frustrated and lonely. Before Marish came into her life, she had no one who really loved her. She was a call girl before she married Jake, a wealthy businessman. Jake did not find this out until after they were married. Jake discovered this through one of his close friends who had used her services in New York. He confronted her and at the time she thought he would divorce her. Surprised, she felt grateful to him when he said he didn't mind. Later, when he told her about his plans for her, she threatened to leave him.

"You can leave anytime you want to," Jake told her, "But you can only take the clothes and other things you brought with you when you came.You signed a prenuptial agreement, along with some other papers."

Esther was horror-struck. She had long ago rid herself of those old clothes and outdated personal items. So she stayed and was allowed to charge anything she wanted to, but could get no cash. She charged everything she could, including stocks and bonds. There would be a time when he would try to get rid of her and she would be ready. Esther started collecting dividends and put the cash into a safe deposit box along with whatever negotiable bonds she could get her hands on. After twenty years of marriage to Jake and making secret deals with most of the businessmen she was forced to sleep with, Esther was herself a millionaire. She continued to use Jake's money to finance her affair with Marish.

Marish was a confused man, His mother had pressed him into marriage with a woman he did not love in Bombay, by threatening to disinherit him from the family fortune. He was a big spender and in debt, way over his head. Esther would buy his clothes and anything he needed with Jake's charge card, but she never gave him any cash. He married the Bombay woman to keep his inheritance, but he left her right there in Bombay.

It didn't make any difference to Esther that Marish was married. Life went on as usual as did their affair.

Eventually Marish requested a transfer to an office in Canada and was assigned there. He continued to fly to his Boston rendezvous.

****

BCS kept taking on additional staff, even though the rumors were flying that the State would be taking over that section.

Steve Beck told Agatha to offer Sheba a promotion and get her back to BCS. He felt that he would be able to control Sheba if she was not with Bob so much of the time. Agatha did as she was told and sent a memo to Sheba that there was a promotion to a new, higher title of Administrative Computer Manager with starting salary $45,000.

When Bob and Sheba discussed the memo, Sheba was very reluctant to return to BCS at any price.

"Bob, they put me through hell. Now, all of a sudden, Agatha wants me back? What's up? Maybe you can find out."

Bob dialed Steve's office. After a few minutes of conversation, he got off the phone.

"Steve said that they are hiring new staff at all levels. BCS will be needing administrative and supervisory staff over the field monitors. The job is yours for the taking, since you have seniority there. Remember you are on loan here. I'll miss working here with you, but we will be together the rest of the time."

"Are you telling me to go back there?"

"I just want you to know I stand behind you, all the way. I wouldn't think of holding you back. Once you get your promotion, I will work to get you back here on a permanent basis in your new title."

Sheba decided to take a calculated risk and return to BCS, on Bob's promise to get her back to WFS.

In the midst of all this hiring, Agatha was sent a new male typist to assist Moreaver and Emmaline, one Geoffry Rozakis.

Moreaver was the head typist and Agatha's secretary. She took advantage of her position, talking down to Geoffry and being very rude to him.

Fed up with her constantly bashing him. Geoffry complained to Agatha about Moreaver.

"Moreaver doesn't know how to talk to people, doesn't know how to train anybody and needs to mind her own business. What I do outside of BCS is my own affair. She has nothing to do with my personal life."

Geoffry was gay and had made the mistake of discussing his personal affairs in the office.

Agatha said sharply to him, "Don't talk to me about Moreaver like that. She is 'saved' and very religious."

"I got news for you," Geoffry answered "Moreaver is nothing and before you get upset, I'd rather terminate this conversation."

With that, Geoffry turned on his heels and walked out of Agatha's office.

All Agatha could say at that moment was "Well!"

Then, recovering, "You come back here and sit down. Don't you walk out of my office like that."

Geoffry turned around, replying, "You can't talk to *me* like that! You gotta' give me respect. I give you and everybody else here respect and I expect the same from you." He went to his desk and sat down.

Everybody's mouth flew open, gaping with surprise.

Agatha never spoke to him after that, the man nauseated her.

Geoffry came into work everyday with his hair sprayed a different color, blond, burgandy, bright red, etc. His face was heavily made up with women's makeup. Underneath the makeup were scores of large red pimples, inundated with pus. His arms were laden with bracelets and chains.

For a while after that things were fairly calm, until one day about lunch time.

Emmaline's boyfriend, Vernon, was calling her before she had a chance to get out the door. She was angry at him and did not wish to speak to him.

Moreaver picked up the phone and looked at Emmaline peculiarly.

Emmaline said, "What's wrong?"

Moreaver put her hand over the mouth piece and said, "It's Vernon."

Emmaline told her to tell him she was out to lunch.

"Oh, no. You know I don't like lying."

Geoffry picked up the phone and said, "I tried to catch Emmaline but she went out to lunch".

Emmaline got her bag and coat, then left. By the time she got downstairs, Vernon was standing there, winded, from running the blocks from Fayette to Church Street. She relented and had lunch with him, letting him foot the bill for coffee and a carton of cigarettes. She was very nervous, she said, and needed them to help her cope with the staff at BCS.

When she got back to the office, as soon as she stepped in the door both Geoffry and Moreaver split. Angry, Emmaline went to the back of the office where they were and blasted them. It was not yet one o'clock.

"You two have got some nerve running out of there like that. I didn't even take my coat off and you don't care if I have to go to the bathroom before starting work."

Geoffry said, "All you had to do was say that."

"That's what I'm saying now."

Geoffry put out his cigarette and went back up front to the office. When Emmaline came back up front, he apologized to her.

"Emmaline, I'm sorry. I had a terrible weekend. It's this guy I was telling you that I go out with on the weekends. I'm in love with the guy."

Some of the pimples had turned into large, red sores.

Emmaline said, "What?"

"Yeah, me and this guy got it on over the weekend."

Emmaline, startled by his candor, asked, "What do you mean, 'got it on'?" She knew what he meant, but pushed him for more details.

"We were making love and he asked me if I would take him back. Now I'm really torn. I'm not the type who can leave my problems at home. I'm sorry. I was thinking about that,'cause I really love the guy. I don't want to have to go through these changes with him anymore."

After that, Geoffry sat at his desk, mooning, as though he were really in love. He sat there staring at the walls, turning various shades of red, running his fingers through his streaked orange hair.

Moreaver returned from lunch and looked at Geoffry. She asked Emmaline, "What's wrong with him?"

Emmaline put both her hands together and lifted them to her cheek in a coy gesture and said, "He's in lo… ove."

At that last statement, Geofrry flushed so deeply that he almost fell out. Emmaline watched him for a few seconds. He looked as though he was about to cry.

Emmaline asked. "What in the world is wrong, Geoffry?"

"Well, when me and my boyfriend were going out, we were real tight for six months. He would always give me excuses, I gotta' do this, I gotta' do that, when all I wanted to do was move out."

Moreaver curious, asked stupidly. "Well, when are you gonna' get married, Geoffry?"

Geoffry, cool, answered, "I'll probably be like my uncle, he's 62 and he's been a batchelor all his life."

Each day when he came in, he had an additional pimple. When he wore a low neckline, it was obvious that his boyfriend had his mouth on Geoffry's neck. Geoffry had several large hickeys there.

Geoffry would tell Emmaline how he dressed up on weekends going to the gay bar where he worked part time. His hair was very long in back, but the front was a little shorter and teased up very high and spikey. The shirts he wore were real long and he wore falsies under them. The patrons would wait to see what he would wear next. When he walked, he twisted his behind and took long strides.

Just before Agatha had him transferred to the Bronx, Geoffry's sores and pimples began to dribble pus. The Commissioner ordered him to get a doctor's note explaining his condition. The other workers complained and started wearing rubber gloves around the office.

Added to that, Kenny was admitted to the hospital and diagnosed as having AIDS. Timmie, his live-in-lover, also had AIDS and was worse off than Kenny. He was so sick, that he couldn't work anymore. With Kenny in the hospital for a long stay, they had to give up their expensive condominium.

Timmie died shortly after Kenny went home to him. Kenny went home to his family in Florida and died there.

Glenda organized a memorial service for Kenny and the people in top management went to the memorial, taking his death badly.

Most of them had had direct or indirect sexual contact with him. The body had been cremated. The mortician refused to embalm the body because he had died of AIDS. They did not want contact with the blood, taking their cue from the physicians and surgeons who refused to operate on AIDS patients because of blood spattering. Kenny's family had wanted a traditional funeral but could not find any mortician to service them, except with cremation.

Even the people who cleaned the bathroom were using rubber gloves up to their elbows. Staff started using plastic gloves to go to the toilet because so many people did not even bother to wash their hands after using the facilities.

****

Violet Grey was one of the newcomers to BCS. Her title, Principle Administrative Associate III, was given to her by a former Center Director. She had wanted the Office Manager's job. The director of the center was a White woman who was having an affair with Violet. The two of them ganged up on the office manager and she transferred out to another location, maintaining her administrative manager title.

Although Violet was married and had five teenaged children, she and the director became lovers. The affair was so intense that it broke up Violet's marriage. When the director went to Europe for a long vacation, Violet's husband went back to her. As soon as the director returned, the husband left again. They began to get sloppy with the affair and several staff members in the local center threatened to bring both of them up on charges.

As a team, Violet and her lover were vicious, unrelenting, obsessive and unforgiving, even when they were dead wrong. The staff was miserable, filing grievance after grievance. The Department of Labor finally ordered a transfer for Violet and arranged for her to go to BCS. She pretended to be sweet and pleasant for a while.

Then Agatha started to brag that Sheba was coming back.She hinted that Sheba would get the Deputy Director position that she, Agatha, had vacated to become the Director.

Violet Gray was sick and tired of hearing how wonderful and sweet Sheba Welters was long before they met. She began to hate the woman's guts, curdling every time someone mentioned Sheba's name. Agatha kept hinting that Sheba would be made the deputy director of BCS. Sean went along with this. If Sean agreed, then Agatha knew that Clovis, who was Sean's immediate boss and lover, would also approve. As far as Violet was concerned, that was never going to happen.

Violet was made the head supervising field monitor. Each supervising field monitor had a field team of six field monitors. Sheba was to start as a supervising field monitor.

When Sheba finally went back to BCS, Violet was ready for her. She had mapped out a perfect strategy, one that always worked. She waited until Sheba had been working in the job for a month and then Violet slowly began to act as a demagogue. Violet downgraded Sheba to everybody, calling her stupid and incompetent, especially to Agatha and her superiors. It was easy to deceive Agatha who had no clue about field or center work.

Violet's goal was to leave Sheba totally friendless. But she had not considered Emmaline. Sheba had befriended Emmaline when she needed a friend, so Emmaline continued to fraternize with Sheba. She enjoyed aggravating Violet and the rest of that clique, who made life miserable for anybody who didn't agree with them.

What Sheba couldn't understand was how Agatha could let Violet tell her that she was incompetent.Violet was new to BCS and WFS, which was new to *everybody*. WFS was still in the testing stages, even as the system was being prepared for installation in the centers. Neither Agatha nor Violet could answer any of Sheba's questions about the work and on occasion, when Violet did answer, she sounded as though she was talking about something other than computers. Either she didn't know anything about the system or she was trying to confuse Sheba.

Needing answers to her questions, Sheba asked to attend the State's WFS courses on maintenance and monitoring of the WFS equipment. Agatha flatly turned down her request.

Sheba had long ago requested and received early hours, 8 a.m. to 3:30 p.m. due to the long ride out to the Island. Bob arrived and left with her. With that in mind, Violet would schedule supervisory meetings twice a week from 3 p.m. to 4 p.m. knowing Sheba was waiting to leave, she would waste time on the telephone to lengthen the meetings to two hours. When Sheba spoke to Agatha, the woman suggested she change her hours to match everybody else's.

In addition to the regular duties that all the other supervising field monitors had, Violet had talked Agatha into assigning Sheba all the projects that were backlogged and need cleaning up. This amounted to a grand total of fourteen extra projects. (After Sheba left the job, those projects were divided amoung ten different people, with one project so complicated they had to put a worker on it full time).

Violet told Agatha vicious lies about the reports Sheba submitted and accused Sheba of putting a 'phantom name' on one report. She stated that Sheba made numerous errors on her reports.

Violet neglected to mention to Agatha that Sheba saved the implementation of the new system in the centers from a gross error of Violet's. Violet had made schedules for the startup dates for the new equipment. She had failed to check her schedule against the previous schedule, thereby sending workers and equipment out to the centers on the wrong dates. Sheba caught Violet's error and instead of bringing it to Agatha's attention, she went to Violet. Violet fixed the error, pretending she had discovered it herself.

When Agatha repeated Violet's lies to Sean, he was calm.

"I've read all the reports of all the supervising field monitors, including Violet Gray. Sheba's reports aren't any worse than anybody else's, in fact, they are a damn sight better than the rest. For two years, I worked with Sheba at WFS and she did excellent work there, reports and everything else. Now you tell me suddenly, she has become incompetent? Get real. Listen to me, it's plain to see what is going down there, If Sheba does not qualify for that deputy director's job, then nobody there does. I have checked out her personnel folder, and she has the background and experience needed for that job. Every position she has held she received outstanding and excellent performance evaluations, from the moment she entered City service. I promise you, I will bring in a total outsider for the job if you and Violet Gray continue with this charade."

Ilene saw Agatha when she came back to her office and decided to ask what had happened at the meeting with Sean.

Agatha wasn't calm enough to talk to her yet, so Ilene told her she would come back later.

Although she wasn't quite ready to take the deputy director postition herself, Ilene wanted Sheba's job and was ready to do a lot of "favors" to get it. In her own words, "I will do anything to get ahead."

Sheba had been Ilene's boss at County Bureau #105 and Ilene was jealous of her even then. The men loved and respected her, because she carried herself with grace. Ilene resented the fact that she was not treated with the same respect.

Ilene had attended the Union's annual party in an outrageous Felix of Hollywood outfit. The staff, including her so-called friends, talked about it for days afterward. With skin-tight pants and a tunic that had long slits up to the arm holes, it clung to her as though someone had saturated her all over with water.

Nellie St. James asked, "What possessed Ilene to wear something like that? Who does she think she is?"

Ray White, sitting in the back with Gertrude Hardwick, said, "Oh, you should have seen that bitch last night. She looked terrible with that tight stuff on. That skin-tight pink and white out-fit with pink and white zebra srtipes. Her shoes were pink with five-inch heels, pink handbag with glitter and she had all this glittering shit on her eyes. And when she walked in, she said loudly, TA DA, I'm here. And everybody just fell out laughing."

After that Ilene lost her credibility.

She was going to move up, no matter what it took to get there. When Sheba left County Bureau #105, Ilene called her to see how she liked working there. Sheba sounded so ecstatic, that Ilene had someone pull strings and she followed Sheba there.

Ilene's jealousy of Sheba never subsided. Once she was ensconced at BCS, the climate there began to change for Sheba. Ilene was like the devil. It was Ilene who introduced hard-core pornograghy to the men and women there.

As soon as Ilene got a chance, she spoke to Agatha. Finding out that nobody at BCS would be getting the deputy director's position, she pushed Agatha to move Sheba out of the supervising field monitor's job. Agatha was reluctant to do so.

"Well, can you get me an appointment with Steve Beck?"

"Why?'

"Maybe if I go over Sean's head, I can get that job."

"I'll try, but Steve is a hard man to bargain with. You'd better have something to offer him in return." Agatha warned. "Something extraordinary."

"I'm always prepared."

"You don't know what you are getting yourself into, Ilene."

"So, he may be a little kinky. I've had men like that before."

Agatha called Steve's office. She was surprised when he agreed to see her that very afternoon. When Ilene heard that, she was exuberant.

In Steve's office, Ilene sat with her legs crossed high, exposing practically every inch of her thigh, high enough for Steve to see she wasn't wearing any underwear.

"What can I do for you?" Steve asked softly.

"I want Sheba Welter's job. Agatha said I had to speak to you. Sean says he has no intentions of removing Sheba from that job."

"Sheba is an excellent worker, she came up through the ranks. From the time she came into the city as an entrance clerk, she has had an excellent work performance record. She's worked hard, studied for the exams and passed them all. Now that she has worked way up to managerial level, you want to take it away from her. Why should I move her and give *you* that position? You can't do what she does. I've seen some of the shit you submitted for lesson plans. You disappear during working hours out in the field. You were supposed to be at an important meeting, and didn't bother to come into work that day nor did you bother to call Agatha. To make things worse, when she called you at home, you were in bed with a man. You let him answer the phone, and when you finally got on, you told Agatha to f—k herself. Yes, I know all about that. I was ready to get rid of you then, but it seems you have some pull. You are what amounts to an unsatisfactory staff member. Why should I move Sheba and give you that position? You can't do what she does." Steve said firmly.

"I can do things she won't do." Ilene's voice took on erotic undertones, uncrossing her legs to give Steve a good look at what she had to offer.

Steve stared at her for a few second without expression, then got up from his chair. He walked around his desk and stood in front of her.

Ilene looked at him and licked her lips, slowly. He unzipped his fly.

"Let's see what you can do. If you do what she won't do for me, I'll give you Sheba's job."

Ilene fell to her knees and performed her heart out. She did all the things that Sheba wouldn't do.

Half an hour later, Steve zipped his fly and returned to his desk. He picked up the phone and dialed Agatha. Her secretary answered.

"Let me speak to Agatha, please."

"Agatha, this is Steve. Ilene is here in my office. She seems to be perfectly qualified to take over Sheba's job as supervising field monitor... Take my word for it... As soon as you can arrange it... I'll expect results in the near future. Do what you have to do."

He hung up and addressed Ilene.

"I expect to be calling you to my office every now and then for 'meetings'. I also have friends and business associates who will need your services occasionally."

Ilene looked startled.

Steve smiled. "I need people like you to help me get favors and build up my power base. There are men and women in top management who need 'relaxation' at times. As soon as Agatha fits you in, be ready to comply, day or night. By the way, I understand you have an 18 year-old daughter. I'd like to meet her some day."

Ilene started to say something.

Steve stared coldly at her. Ilene's waist-long, bleached blond hair was damp with sweat and hanging limply. Her makeup was smeared, her dress wrinkled and she needed a shower.

"You wanted in, you got in. I like and admire Sheba. She's a decent, hardworking woman, and much to my regret, not generous with her body, like you are. But, as you say, there are certain things she won't do and you will. Agatha expects you back at the office now."

Steve turned to the papers on his desk, and Ilene knew she was dismissed. She got up and walked slowly to the door, feeling grossly humilated. There was no turning back, she would do anything to get ahead even sacrifice her daughter, if that's what it took. This was all part of the game.

****

Rafael had found out which office Sheba transferred to and followed her there as security chief. He still couldn't get anywhere with her, but wanted to be near her.

He would arrive at six each morning to check out the building. While he checked out each floor, the cleaning men, Tony and Jerry, did their jobs.

Rafael would complete his morning check by the time Sheba arrived and wait downstairs by the entrance for her arrival. The other security guard sat at a desk by the entrance checking people as they came into the building.

When Rafael noticed that Sheba never used the elevator, he questioned her about it.

She looked at him curiously before answering him.

"That elevator looks and feels like a tomb. It takes from ten to twenty minutes just to get to the third floor. My heart starts beating like a hammer when it takes too long, because I'm afraid it's stuck. There aren't any windows in there, it's all steel and sealed in, and very dark just like a tomb."

Rafael laughed and said, "I'll take you to your floor anytime you want."

"Forget it. Being on the elevator with you isn't going to make that elevator go faster or more pleasant." Sheba answered.

He laughed again, but Sheba walked up to the third floor anyway.

The day after Ilene's visit to Steve Beck's office Agatha was waiting in her office when Sheba arrived at 8:30. Once Sheba settled into working on reports, Agatha sent Emmaline to get her.

As soon as Sheba saw the expression on Agatha's face, she knew she was in for *another* very unpleasant experience.

"Yes, Agatha?"

"I've been hearing a lot of bad things about you." Agatha had a mean look on her face.

As she waited for Agatha to continue, Sheba decided that if Agatha made her angry today, she would transfer out of this section as soon as she left this meeting.

"From where?" Sheba asked.

"From center directors, center staff and your co-workers."

Agatha was lying, center directors did not contact her directly. Neither did any of the local staff.They always spoke to Violet Gray, Agatha wouldn't take complaints like that. Sheba tuned her out, there was no reason for her to stay in an acrimonious atmosphere such as this. It was making her sick just to sit here and listen to this disturbed woman, who was merely spouting Violet's lies. Whenever she asked either of them a question about the new system, neither of them could give an intelligent answer and Sheba would have to call someone outside of BCS. When Agatha had been told by Violet that Sheba called for out side help, Agatha ordered Sheba to stop going to other agencies.

They continued to refuse to send her for additonal training, refused to answer her questions, did not want her to get outside help, did not want to listen to reason.

"I pulled back your promotional papers and I'm taking you out of the position of supervising field monitor. You will stay here in the office with me, doing special projects."

"Oh no, I won't. I won't stay here in this office with you and do anything."

Agatha was shocked at Sheba's reaction.

"Your husband won't be able to help you in this case and I will make trouble for you wherever you go." Agatha was getting meaner.

Sheba turned and walked out of Agatha's office and into her own. She was visibly upset and shaken. Bob was at a meeting and could not be reached. She started throwing away the work that had taken her years to develop and create, volumes upon volumes, into the trash, unaware that the BCS buzzards were just waiting to zoom in on whatever she was naive enough to leave behind.

Moments after she went through the door at five o'clock, they flocked over her abandoned belongings like vultures over a body. Each person went away from the dumpster clutching book and papers grinning like Count Dracula after feasting on a helpless victims blood.

Violet Gray and Ilene Levison could not hide their exuberance. Sheba was definitely out of the running for the deputy director's job and Ilene knew she would be getting Sheba's job.

Rafael was not in the office when this went down. By the time he returned to work, Sheba had already quit and packed her things. Although Rafael cared a great deal for Sheba, he realized he still reported to Agatha. He asked Sheba if he could do anything to help her, then he stood by with Emmaline watching Sheba prepare to leave.

It hurt him, but what could he do? Agatha and the others had ganged up on her. Most of the sabotage that befell Sheba was carefully planned and executed. The person ultimately responsible was Agatha Fluddrucker.

Sheba was the most decent person, man or woman, whom he had ever met, and he had traveled far since leaving Sanga Mara nearly 25 years ago.

Some of the women who were jealous of Sheba accused her of putting on airs and called her a variety of names "Miss Goody Two-Shoes", "Prude" as well as the usual "old fashioned" behind her back. Agatha called her a prima donna to her face and she said she carried herself like a product of "Prudence's Private Finishing School." Sheba's lack of a college degree, gave Agatha yet another excuse not to give her a promotion.

After Sheba left, Rafael hung around to give the building another check. The other guard had left earlier and he was doing him a favor.

Karen Leach came out of her office, heading into the ladies' room. Rafael stood watching her as she swished away from him. Her hips were undulating from side to side in a sensuous roll. When she was out of sight, he turned and rang for the elevator.It was late, almost six o'clock. Karen had to stay until transmissions were completed, occasionally until seven. She was probably getting ready to go home now, maybe he should wait for her. He lost that thought quickly. His girlfriend was waiting for him, he was in hurry to eat the big dinner she had promised to cook for him. Her mouth would drive him crazy if he was late.

Rafael was losing patience, the damn elevator was taking its time, even longer than usual. Just as he started to walk down, it arrived. He stepped in, alone in that box. A weird feeling crept over him and he couldn't wait to get down to the first floor. Sheba's words rang in his ears. "That elevator is like a tomb, no windows, all heavy steel." Rafael felt the space closing in on him, making him claustrophobic.

"Hell!" His anxiety was beginning to overwhelm him. It was taking too long to get moving. He glanced at his watch. It was now six-thirty. His hands began to shake as he pressed the alarm. He waited, but no one came. After a few moments he laid on the alarm.

Suddenly the lights went out in the elevator and the alarm stopped ringing. He was in pitch blackness, the air no longer circulating. Panic enveloped him, as he remembered that the electricity shut down at seven-thirty. Rafael frantically pressed all the buttons he could feel in the dark. Nothing happened.

Rafael stayed in that dark, desolate elevator all night long. Reportedly, Sheba's words came back to him, sounding hollow and deadly. "It's like a tomb." He pictured himself found dead of a heart attack or from lack of air on this damned elevator. A tomb, *his* tomb. Something warm and wet was going down his legs. It suddenly dawned on him that he was *urinating on himself.* Laughing bitterly, he recalled how many times he accused someone else of being so scared that they pissed on themselves. His laughter was shortlived as he came back to the moment with an absolute terror smothering him.

When they found Rafael in the morning, alive, his eyes looked as though they were about to pop out of his head. The elevator reeked of urine which covered the entire floor. He was sent to the nearest hospital for three days.

Rafael never entered into that elevator again.

****

When Sheba left BCS, Emmaline felt as though she had lost the only friend she'd ever had in this world. The relationship she had with Agatha was not really fulfilling. So when she became aware of a man who watched her steadily each morning at the restaurant where she ate breakfast, she was thrilled.

One morning he introduced himself as Jessup Woodstock and paid for her breakfast. She let him, and after that, it became a daily ritual. Emmaline and Jessup drifted into an affair.

Emmaline told Sheba about Jessup. Sheba had given her the unlisted home phone number. Emmaline waited five months before calling Sheba, then started laying all of her problems on her. Emmaline complained about Agatha, the staff at BCS, her new landlord and Jessup. She claimed she didn't love Jessup, but wanted advice as to how to hook him into marriage.

"I wouldn't know how to "hook" anybody into marriage, Emmaline."

"You hooked your husband." Emmaline retorted.

"Bob and I are very much in love. He asked me to marry him. I didn't have to "hook" him. I don't want anyone I have to stalk or hunt down."

Two months later, Emmaline was back on the phone with Sheba, saying she was pregnant by Jessup.

She had informed Agatha who demanded that Emmaline terminate the pregnancy, stating that her job was on the line. The truth was that Agatha couldn't stand the thought of being involved with a pregnant woman.

Emmaline, who was now 42 years old, claimed she did not want the baby, just as she did not want her first child, a daughter who was now a grown woman addicted to crack.

Speaking to Sheba on the phone, Emmaline sounded distraught.

"Look, Sheba, what would you do in my place?"

"Emmaline, I would never be in your place." Sheba answered.

"Why not?" Emmaline sounded resentful.

"Because I believe in abstinence from intimacy when single. I practiced that way of life between marriages, in spite of the fact that many men and some women told me I would go out of my mind."

"But suppose you did get into this situation?" Emmaline pressed for an answer.

"Then I would have to accept my predicament."

"What do you mean?" Emmaline was getting more frustrated.

"You may not want to hear this, but I don't have a magic cure for you. First of all, your body is accustomed to a certain behavior pattern and unless you went into deep therapy, there isn't anything I can say to change your habits overnight. You started in with a stranger, knowing that he could be married or have AIDS or even be a pervert. It was your choice, just as it was his choice. You were both consenting adults. He may never marry you, baby or not. The law says he doesn't even have to take responsibility for that baby since you are not his wife." Sheba was firm and Emmaline knew she was right, but the truth hurt more than she cared to admit.

"What should I do?" Emmaline persisted. She wanted Sheba to take the blame for her actions.

"Ask GOD." Sheba answered.

"How?" Emmaline sounded desperate.

"Say, GOD grant me the serenity to accept the things I cannot change, courage to change the things I can and wisdom to know the difference. That's not something *I* made up and I am not sure who did. Maybe it will help you."

Although Emmaline resented hearing the truth from Sheba, she still called her, spending hours on the phone with her. Deep down, her unhappiness and misery rumbled around inside of her.

Finally, feeling strongly that she had to hurt Sheba in some way, she dialed Sheba's telephone number, When Sheba answered the phone, Emmaline hung up without a word.

At first, Emmaline would call Sheba (with prodding from Agatha) to find out what her plans were for the future. Agatha wanted to know if Sheba planned to make big trouble for her. She knew that what she had done to Sheba was illegal. When Emmaline found out that Sheba was not suffering and had no plans for a lawsuit, it made Emmaline envious. She was jealous because Sheba had a happy life with her husband, daughter and grandchildren. Sheba seemed to have no complaints about the way things were going in her life. Emmaline wanted Sheba to do something to hurt Agatha.

Seeing that this was not about to happen, Emmaline started making anonymous calls in between the regular calls she made to Sheba. She needed the regular calls, because she could purge herself of all the gruesome things she had been through in her life. It was like a confession to a minister. Sheba would not repeat a confidence, Emmaline knew this for a fact. The soul cleansing feeling was a catharsis each time she told Sheba about her past life.

As for Sheba, those anonymous calls had no particular regularity and at that time were only occasional. So Sheba felt no reason to be anxious.

When the telephone calls became more frequent, then doggedly persistant, Bob called the telephone company. They claimed there wasn't anything they could do about the calls, so he and Sheba had the number changed on the line. She gave the number only to her Aunt Hetty and Bob's parents, Donna and the children lived with her and Bob. No anonymous calls for three months. Then Sheba called Emmaline and gave her the new number.

That's when the anonymous calls got hot and heavy.

At five a.m., the phone rang. Bob picked it up. Over in Harlem, Emmaline gloated wickedly as she let it ring once and then replaced her handset in its cradle. She pictured Sheba's frustration then got out of bed to prepare for work.

Agatha expected Emmaline to be in the office very early in the morning. The two of them snorted coke together in Agatha's office. Then, if Agatha felt like it, they would go into the bathroom for a quick sex fix. If anyone came in, they were in a closed toilet booth, pretending only one person was in there, Emmaline got to work and decided to call Sheba again. This time, she wanted to speak to her and find out if she suspected who was making the harrassment calls. When she dialed the number, the phone kept ringing. There was no cessation, even that damned answering machine did not come on. She hung up and dialed again. The phone just rang. Emmaline dialed Sheba five times or more during the day. The more she dialed, the more frightened she became. She left work early that day.

For the next few weeks, her fright grew into terror and panic. Emmaline tried everyday several times a day for three weeks to get Sheba without success. Now she was certain that Sheba knew it was her making the harrassing calls. What she didn't know was what Sheba was going to do about the situation. Emmaline and Agatha both believed Sheba had some kind of extraordinary powers to make things happen to people.

Agatha thought it was Sheba's mysterious powers that were making BCS fall apart and allowing the State a full takeover. Sheba had told Emmaline that BCS staff were untrained and unknowledgeable just as she'd told Agatha before she left. It was no secret, the entire staff fumbled and bumbled along. Violet Gray could have arranged for further training, but instead chose to pretend to have the knowledge she needed to succeed. She chose to point fingers at Sheba, not aware that the State administrators were doing some indepth checking on her and other staff.

Still Emmaline blamed Sheba because she had left BCS. Agatha was giving Emmaline a hard time in their love-hate relationship. Emmaline did not want Sheba to call Gertrude Hardwick and discover that Emmaline was feeding Sheba certain information. Gertrude had told Emmaline that if she found out that she, Emmaline, was talking to Sheba, that she would kill her ass and Gertrude was plenty mean enough to kill. No telling what that crazy Agatha would do.

Emmaline realized at that point that she was in big trouble. She sat down on the edge of her bed and tears rolled out of her sad, dreary eyes, which blatantly revealed her miserable life.

The next time Emmaline called Sheba, she found that the number had been changed again and was still unlisted. She sent Sheba a letter, begging her to call. Sheba didn't call. She had had enough of Emmaline, now knowing it was Emmaline who was responsible for aggravating her with all those harassing calls. There wasn't anything the woman could say to her that would convince her to resume their friendship. If it weren't for Donna, the children and Bob, she would have had to go under a doctor's care. It hadn't been easy walking away from a well paying job, in fact, it was devastating. But staying would have been worse.

Then, suffering from her job loss, she would listen to Emmaline's constant complaining. She began to feel as though she was completely submerged in Emmaline's complaints. When she found out that her harrasser was Emmaline, Sheba was thoroughly disgusted with her. She never bothered to speak to her again.

<u>1989</u>

Emmaline's dilemma

Emmaline was deep in the throes of the misery that she had created herself. She knew that she had caused Sheba a lot of aggravation that she did not deserve, making those harrassing calls to her home. But Sheba had everything that Emmaline wanted for herself, a good husband, a beautiful daughter, grandchildren and a wonderful home on the Island. Although Sheba invited her there, Emmaline had never shown up. She went by there in Jessup's car one day, telling him "White folks live there." They sat there, looking at the house, until a police car with two mean-looking policemen asked if they were lost. Emmaline said they were just looking at the ocean.

"This is private property, m'am, it's best you move on."

Emmaline never went back there. She felt like a lost soul, no friends, no decent family to speak of, no man of her own (all the good men belonged to somebody else), not even a job that she liked.

She had started a lawsuit against Agatha for cruel and inhumane treatment and sexual harrassment. Sheba had suggested to Emmaline many times that she try to find something else while she still had a job.

Emmaline's standard reply was, "I just can't jump up and leave here like you did, I don't have anyone to take care of me. That's the same way I left home. I couldn't take no more of my mother, I couldn't take no more of my brothers. I couldn't take no more of the people down south. I started runnin' ever since I was a young girl, and I'm tired of it. I'm *tired* of it, I'm tired of runnin' all my life. Since I can remember, I was runnin' from the fact. I just don't want people all the time deceiving me. Maybe I don't have enough get-up-and-go to get what I need. But I am tired of being out there on the street. I don't have the guts anymore to do all the things I should do for myself."

****

<u>1939</u>

The History of Emmaline

Emmaline's untimely birth took place in Mississippi, in 1939. Her mother, Cissy Mcgee, had tried desperately to abort the pregnancy, but failed miserably. Emmaline was determined to be born. On her last attempt, when Cissy almost killed herself, she gave up and let it happen.

Cissy had given birth to seven other children before Emmaline was born and had given away five of them. Cissy tried to give away all of them, but ran out of takers. She wasn't sure who the fathers were.

At first Cissy had given Emmaline to Cynthia, the sister of the man she declared was Emmaline's father. Then she changed her mind. She decided to take Emmaline back because she was a girl and Cissy would need someone to do the housework for her.Cynthia, Emmaline's aunt, had taken 6 month-old Emmaline to a bar, where upon Cynthia got herself very drunk. Detectives came into the bar and took the baby right out of Cynthia's arms.

Later, Emmaline would say, "out of the frying pan, into the fire." Back to Cissy she went.

Cissy's resentment of the baby continued for the rest of Emmaline's unnatural life. Although born healthy, all the torment, anguish, abuse of all types and heartache that she had to endure made Emmaline one very mentally and emotionally disturbed person.

Fortunately for Emmaline, she was not overtly dysfunctional,but only after getting to know her would most people become aware of her instability.

Emmaline's childhood was intensely traumatic and extremely miserable. Cissy didn't want Emmaline around, and her two half brothers hated her as well, systematically raping her every chance they got. Cissy knew what was going on, but the boys took their attitude from her, she brutalized Emmaline every day in different ways.

They would all steal from Cissy so she began putting locks everywhere. All of the rooms were locked except the children's bedrooms and the kitchen. The kitchen cabinets and the refrigerator were locked. Cissy would leave their food out on the kitchen table, the morning's breakfast, three brown paper bags for school lunch plus three plates for dinner. Cissy would cook the food in the morning and leave it out in the open on the plates for the children's evening meal.

Sometimes the food would be rotten from hot weather. Even with that, if Emmaline got home from school a little late, her share of the dinner would be gone. Her brothers would eat everything in sight. The neighbors felt sorry for her and fed her. If it hadn't been for their help, Emmaline would have starved to death.

The brown paper bags had the children's names on them and were left on the table with the other food. One morning, the two boys, Lionel and Fletcher, got up early and beat her into the kitchen. All of the breakfast food was gone, including Emmaline's. She had overslept because they had kept her awake most of the night, taking turns raping her.

The dinner plates weren't there either. Running late, Emmaline grabbed the lunch bag left for her, and began the long trek to school. On the way her stomach started growling at her because it was so empty. She anxiously opened the lunch bag, reached in and pulled out a hand filled with roaches. Some of them started to crawl up her arm. Emmaline screamed, throwing the bag to the ground. Her half brothers had stolen her lunch too.

Emmaline just sat down on the edge of the road and cried, too disgusted to go on. She wanted to die, right then and there. Her two half brothers were so mean and evil that Emmaline wondered if GOD was really there. If He was there, how could He let her family treat her this way? Why didn't He stop them? Why didn't He make them all drop dead?

She was so hungry now that she felt sick. With no breakfast, no lunch and no prospects for dinner, her head felt woozy at the thought of going to school without any food. The thought of no dinner after all that she had gone through the previous night and this morning made her think seriously of killing herself. This happened too often to her.

She stopped complaining to Cissy. Her mother would beat her everytime she complained, getting great pleasure out of abusing Emmaline. Then if she complained about what Fletcher and Lionel did to her, they would beat her too.

The abuse didn't stop in the privacy of the house. Cissy beat Emmaline in public too. When Emmaline was 6 years old, her mother took her on the bus to go shopping for school clothes. She didn't want any of her children wearing rags to school. After all neighbors would talk. On the bus, her mother met a friend and they started chatting. As they talked, the woman noticed Emmaline staring at her and listening to the conversation, which had turned quite obscene. She signaled Cissy, and when her mother saw her staring, she slapped Emmaline across the face so hard that she started screaming at the top of her lungs.

The bus driver stopped the bus and made Cissy take Emmaline off of the bus. For that, Cissy gave Emmaline a terrible beating right there on the street.

When Emmaline was 7 years old, Cissy decided that all of her children needed a 'good cleaning out'. They each received a huge megadose of castor oil simultaneously. What logic prompted her mother to do this, Emmaline never knew. But there was only one toilet. All three children felt the call to nature at the same time. Emmaline beat the other two into the bathroom, leaving the boys in agony.

Cissy called to her.

"Emmaline!"

"Yes'm?"

"Bring yo' ass out of there, right now!"

"I ain't finished yet, Maw." Emmaline called back, right in the middle of a bowel movement.

Cissy turned to the boys and said, "Y'all can shit on the floor. When you are finished, leave it right there cause when that hussy comes outten' the toilet, she's gonna' clean it all up."

Both brothers pulled their pants down and had full bowel movements. When Emmaline finished with the bathroom, her mother made her clean up the entire mess.

Some of Emmaline's beatings stemmed from the fact that she looked like her 'no-good' father. Her mother was constantly reminding her that she looked 'just like him' and would never amount to anything. Cissy also said that Emmaline was stubborn and no good, just like her daddy.

Occasionally, right after one of these beatings, Cissy would make Emmaline scratch her head. What Cissy's head needed was a washing instead of a scratching. At 7, Emmaline was not very tall and her mother had to sit on the floor to get her head scratched. If Emmaline did not want to work with the dirty, smelly head that had not been washed in months, she got still another beating.

After the beating, Emmaline refused to speak to her mother for two or three days. Angry, Cissy would beat her again. Emmaline would then refuse to eat. Worried that Emmaline would get sick and die, Cissy would fix Emmaline's favorite foods. If the child was hungry enough, she ate the food, then the cycle would start all over again. Beating Emmaline was her mother's favorite pastime. If Emmaline's brothers lied about her, she got another beating. Her small body was covered with permanent scars.

The subsequent six years followed the same general pattern. Her half brothers celebrated her thirteenth birthday by raping her. It was about that time that she had her first menstruation cycle.

Nine months later, the birth of her daughter took her and everyone by surprise. Cissy had told her babies came from trees. Special trees. She had no prenatal care, therefore the doctors had no way of knowing that Emmaline was having a breach baby.

The doctors opted for a natural birth and did not administer an anesthetic. The birth was also very dry and took two days of intense labor pains to deliver the baby. The attending physicians had to turn the baby around inside of her, pulling and snatching with their big hands in her small body. The unbearable pain almost killed both Emmaline and the baby.

Fortunately for Emmaline, the baby was very small, four pounds and six ounces. She prayed to God not to let her give birth to any more babies.

Through all of this, Cissy never visited her at the hospital. She was furious because she had to pay the hospital expenses and was ordered by the Sheriff to take both of the children back into the house with her. Emmaline stayed in the hospital for five weeks, hemorrhaging profusely, intermittently. Even when she stopped, her mother refused to take her and the baby back into the house.

Finally, the authorities told Cissy they would put her in jail if she continued to refuse to bring the children home.Ultimately, Emmaline was *her* responsibility.

Emmaline would have preferred to stay elsewhere, if she were given a choice. She would never forget the day that Cissy found out that she was pregnant. Cissy beat Emmaline for being pregnant, then allowed her half brothers to beat Emmaline to a bloody pulp, for accusing them of raping her. Then, Cissy threw the pulverized child out of the house with a dollar and a loaf of bread.

"Don't you come back here, you low-down, good-for-nothing hussy." Cissy snarled at her.

Crying hysterically, Emmaline dragged her brutally bruised body down the porch stair steps to the dirt road near the house. A car was moving toward her. All she could think of was that she wanted very badly to die, to be rid of her cruel mother and her brutal brothers. She dragged herself out into the middle of the road and lay there, waiting, hoping to die.

The driver, a middle-aged Black man, saw her and stopped in time. He and his wife got out of the car. Without hesitating, they put Emmaline into the car and drove her to the nearest hospital. They brought her to the emergency room and quickly left, not wanting to get involved in whatever mess the child's situation would create.

The hospital staff became involved immediately. They called the police, who contacted Emmaline's mother. Cissy vehemently denied ever laying a hand on the child. She swore she had no idea who the father of the unborn child was, in fact, she said, she didn't even know Emmaline was pregnant.

The hospital administrators told Cissy that until she found out who was responsible for Emmaline's condition, she would be held responsible for all the bills as well as her physical being. The Sheriff said that if there were any additional bruises, Cissy would go to jail. That threat saved Emmaline from furthur beatings. Cissy had a mind to give Emmaline the beating of her life when she got out of the hospital, but the Sheriff's promise put an end to that idea.

When Cissy came home from the hospital that day, she called Fletcher and Lionel to the living room.

"Which one of you niggers knocked up Emmaline?" Her voice boomed out at them. She was a tough-looking woman, taller than either of her sons, huskily built, with muscular arms from lifting heavy boxes at the factory.

Both sets of male eyes grew large and frightened. Fletcher was now 17 and Lionel was 15. They pointed at each other. Cissy towered over the both of them and much stronger than the two of them put together, hollered "Don't you bastards play with me, I ain't in no playin' mood."

She grabbed Fletcher and whacked him on the side of his head so hard that it stunned him.

"Lionel didn't want to get hit, but he did it to Emmaline and asked me not to tell on him."

Lionel, scared out of his wits, said sobbing, "He's lyin' Ma. He's the one who did it to Emmaline... He said he would kill me if I told on him."

Cissy looked from one to the other.

"I'm gonna get the truth here, tonight. Y'all both strip down."

"O.K. Fletcher, you're the oldest. *Come here.*"

Fletcher hesitated a second too long.Cissy reached out with the belt and cracked him across his mouth. Blood gushed out as he screamed.

"Mama, wait, I'll tell you everything." He talked and talked, until his swollen mouth ran dry, the blood gush slowing to a drip down his bare body.

"You two low-down dirty skunks, because of the two of you, I gotta' take my hard earned money and pay a big hospital bill. I ought to have your asses thrown in jail. It's a crying' shame. Both of you are gettin' your lazy screwin' asses out of school. You are both going to get jobs and pay that damn hospital bill, for the baby's upkeep, for Emmaline's upkeep and for your own upkeep. There are jobs down at the factory for the both of you."

Lionel, quivering, said, "I ain't 16 yet."

Cissy raised the belt, and whacked him brutally across the mouth.

"Don't talk back to me. You ain't sixteen, yet. You'll be lucky to live to get to sixteen, at the rate you and your brother is going. Why didn't you think about how young you are, when you started screwin' your little sister. I bet you felt like a grown man then."

Cissy beat them both within an inch of their lives, the boys' faces and bodies were a bloody mess. That didn't stop her from taking them out of school the next day and to the factory with her to get jobs. They were given the most menial positions available. She took their entire paychecks, except for a dollar each.

Cissy warned them to never touch Emmaline again in any way or they would go to jail. She wasn't about to take responsibility for their crimes.

Grudgingly, Cissy brought Emmaline home from the hospital when the time came. She couldn't wait for Emmaline to reach 16. Cissy had bought a little house for Emmaline and the baby in order to get rid of them. She could not stand to look at her granddaughter because she resembled Fletcher so much.

When Emmaline's daughter, Lillie, was 6 months old, she developed a fever, throwing up constantly. One of her neighbors told her to take the baby to the hospital. Emmaline was reluctant to do this, remembering her own stay there. Finally, unable to endure the baby's illness anymore, she took the baby there finally realizing that Lillie really needed to be there. Immediately, they put her into an oxygen tent, keeping her there until she was well. Cissy took the baby away from Emmaline at that point and refused to give her back to Emmaline.

Although her mother was supporting her, Emmaline could no longer bear being treated so cruelly. She wanted a better life, so the first chance she got she ran away to Mega City. In Mega City she obtained a position as a live-in-maid as soon she arrived from the south.

She saved her money diligently, and when her daughter was 2 years old, Emmaline went back down south to try to get her back. The White lawyer she consulted told her, "Why don't you let them keep her? They've had her since she was a little baby and they're doing a fine job." He ignored all the things she had told him that her mother and brothers had done to her, she knew he did not believe a word she said.

Emmaline left the lawyer's office in tears. Every time she went to Cissy's house to see her daughter, she was told Lillie wasn't there. When Emmaline asked where could a 2 year old child be *by herself*, Cissy would threaten her.

Later, Emmaline was to find out where Lillie had been when she came to see her daughter.

When Lillie was 25 years old, she came to Mega City looking for her mother. She was a hard-core dope addict. Lillie told Emmaline that she held her responsible for her dependency on drugs. She said that she should not have given birth to her leaving her in that house full of 'sick people'. Emmaline tried to explain what had happened, but Lillie only knew she was really hurting and she blamed her mother.

Lillie was in tears when she told Emmaline about the closet.

"You know everytime you came to see me, they tied me up and gagged me with a towel then threw me in the closet. Fletcher and Lionel told me that if I told anybody what they did to me or that I wanted to be with my momma, they would kill me. I even had to ask permission to use the toilet. Sometimes they would say 'no', and I would make in my pants and they would beat me."

Emmaline hung her head down when she heard this, because she knew Lillie was telling the truth. She too had gone through some terrible times because of her mother and brothers. That day when Lillie was 2 and Emmaline tried to retrieve her child, she had to go back to Mega City. She found that she had even lost her live-in job, and was now homeless. Emmaline had to walk the streets of Mega City in the pitch-black dark of night, not knowing where she was going.

When daylight came and the sun rose, she came across a park with wooden benches. To Emmaline, those wooden benches looked like the best of soft mattresses. She sat there, upright, and fell asleep. When she woke up, an elderly Black man was sitting on the bench with her. He was watching her and it gave her a start.

"Don't be afraid, I was just sitting here looking out for you. Mega City is one place you got to keep your wits about you and your eyes open. Unless you are home in your own bed and even then you got to be careful." The old man laughed when Emmaline looked at him with a puzzled look on her face. Answering the look, he said, "It's true."

"I ain't sayin' it ain't true, but you could be a crook yourself." Emmaline was not angry, but she was so used to rough talk, that she did not know how to be tactful.

"Believe me, Miss, I was only trying to help you. I'm 74 years old, I gets my pension checks from my city job, plus I gets my Social Security checks each month. I don't have to ask nobody for nuthin' and I sho' don't have to steal from you. Besides, you don't look like you got anything to steal, 'ceptin' yo' self, of course."

He smiled gently at her, hoping to make friends with her.He guessed that she could use a friend, too.The old man was determined not to let this opportunity slip by, for both their sakes. This girl had a battered suitcase and a small cheap pocketbook. She looked like she desperately needed a place to stay. Well, he had an extra room she could have if she wanted to stay with him.

"You sho' right about that. I ain't got nothing nobody would want to steal," she answered sadly.

"Look, young lady, I ain't tryin' to be fresh or anything, but if you ain't got no place to stay, right now, I got a room you can rent for very little," he blurted.

She looked at him with sad, miserable eyes.

"I only got nine dollars and thirty-five cents to my name and I have to get something to eat out of that, before I starve to death", Emmaline answered in a small, pitiful voice.

"Tell you what, I won't charge you any rent until you get a job."

"I don't know you. I don't know anything about you," she answered in a firm voice.

"I don't know you either and I sho' don't know anything about you. My name is Truman Delmar and I live right across the street, over there, in that red brick house on the first floor. I used to live on the top floor but since I retired, I moved downstairs to make life a little easier. Everybody in the neighborhood knows me. Go ask any of these store owners, they can tell you all about me. I been around here, a long, long time." Truman tried to smile his best and most agreeable smile at Emmaline.

She looked him up and down, openly. Hell, she thought to herself, I got nothing to lose but my life and that ain't worth much. "Okay," she said reluctantly," But the very first time you give me any trouble at all, I'm out of there.I am sick and tired of taking shit from you men, young or old."

"You musta' seen some mighty hard times, young lady. At this time of my life, all I want is some peace and quiet, so don't you give *me* any trouble either. I can help you out with a place to stay and you will be company for me. I get very lonely sometimes," Trumans eyes were sad and pleading.

He rose to leave and Emmaline picked up her belongings. They walked side-by-side to his apartment.

The apartment was tidy and roomy, but sparsely furnished. The livingroom had only a sofa, a reclining armchair and a small television set.

"How do you like it?" He studied Emmaline's face for a reaction.

"It's just fine. Show me the room *I* sleep in."

He took her down a long hall. The first door was the bathroom. That was big too, with a old-fashioned bathtub and sink. Next was a tremendous bedroom, with a huge bed which had mahogany headboards.

"This is where I sleep." He lingered there for a moment, waiting for her to say something.

"This is really nice," she said sincerely. Everything was so clean.

Truman smiled, pleased at Emmaline's remark. He knew that they would get along just fine.

Emmaline's room was slightly smaller than Truman's, but still large enough. The bed was a single bed, but it was clean.

"I can't stand a dirty house, you will have to keep this room clean or else we won't get along. Anyplace in this apartment that you make a mess, you gonna' have to clean it up. I don't be cleaning up behind anybody. If you don't like cleaning your own mess, you might as well leave right now."

Emmaline was happy to have a place to stay, so happy that she kissed Truman on the cheek. The old man was thrilled. After that, he began to fantasize about Emmaline. They hit it off quite well and when she began to clean the whole apartment and cook for him, Truman was in ecstasy.

They stayed together for two years, Emmaline catering to his basic needs, he in turn supporting her and letting her have some spending money.

****

1959

Emmaline's new husband

In 1959, Truman Delmar died. He had designated Emmaline as his beneficiary on his bank account and his insurance policy. She was exuberant, only grieving for Truman long enough to get his funeral out of the way. The coffin was the cheapest she could buy.

After getting the insurance check and cleaning out the late Truman Delmar's bank accounts, Emmaline immediately packed her belongings and headed for the south, to show off her new-found fortune.

In Mississippi, Emmaline met and married Eric Spenser, a smooth-talking Black dude who was determined to get every penny of the money Emmaline was flashing around.

Eric, though smooth as glass, was an average-looking man who swept Emmaline off her feet because he was the first young, unrelated male who paid any attention to her. After they married, he turned into a beast.

No more Mr. Nice Guy.

Eric forced Emmaline to sign over her house to him by beating her senseless every night. All the money Emmaline recieved from Truman Delmar's death was drained. Eric forced her into unspeakable sexual acts. In the end, he was worse than her mother and brothers.

Once again, Emmaline escaped from this new purgatory, and ran away to Mega City. She managed to get another live-in-job, this time as a domestic worker in Scarsdale. The White couple treated her badly and eventually refused to pay her.

At a loss as to how she could get her money, she called her mother. Cissy called Emmaline's husband, Eric. He drove up to Scarsdale and demanded her money. One of his disreputable looking friends came into the house with him, while two others waited outside with the motor running.

The White couple afraid of what these Black people would do to them paid Emmaline her money, breathing a sigh of relief when Emmaline packed her bags and left.

Emmaline the essential dreamer, got carried away with herself and the thought that Eric really loved her because he had come to her rescue. She forgot all about the beatings and the other abuse, and went back to Mississippi with him.

This time, Eric daily used Emmaline for a punching bag. He made her get a job to support him and buy him a new car. She never tried to defend herself and he continued to beat her. Emmaline was deathly afraid of him, fearing that each beating would be her last. She knew that if she stayed with him, one day he would kill her.

Managing to save a few dollars from each paycheck, Emmaline took the money she accumulated and returned to Mega City. She was fascinated by everything there. Determined to get her life in order now, she applied for a cleaning job with the telephone company. They hired her and she found an apartment she could afford, buying inexpensive new furniture.

Unfortunately, Emmaline was lonely and wanting to have someone to communicate with, she wrote her to her husband, Eric. He didn't answer her letter or wait for an invitation to come to Mega City. Eric grabbed the next train out of Mississippi, to carry him back into the arms of his miserable wife. There Emmaline was again, supporting her abusive husband.

It wasn't enough that Eric abused Emmaline and forced her to support him, but he insisted that his cousin, Ruby, live there with them. The woman came to Mega City on the pretext of attending a nursing school. The extra bedroom in Emmaline's apartment gave Eric an excuse to allow Ruby to stay with them. Because Ruby was his first cousin, Emmaline gave in and let her stay there.

A week after Ruby thrust her presence into Emmaline's apartment, Ruby showed her utter contempt for the woman who was giving her a place to stay and food to eat.

When Emmaline got to work that particular day, she felt ill and returned home.When she opened her bedroom door to lay down in *her* bed, it was already occupied by Eric and Ruby, deep in the throes of very intimate passion. Ruby, who saw Emmaline first, froze. Eric had his back to Emmaline and hadn't seen her yet.Emmaline darted over to the bed and started to grab the woman. Eric grabbed Emmaline.

"What the hell you doin' in my bed?" Emmaline's jaw dropped when she realized that the woman was her husband's first cousin.

Flashing through Emmaline's mind was the fact that Ruby was always home no matter what time Emmaline came home from work. Still, she hadn't had a clue that the woman was *willingly* going with her own first cousin.

Angry because she had caught them, and in *her* bed, she couldn't understand why they hadn't used Ruby's room. The two were hot and heavy into what they were doing and Eric had not wanted to stop. Emmaline grabbed the hussy and tried to beat her. Then Eric started to beat Emmaline, pulling her hair and tearing all of her clothes off her body, then beating her to a bloody pulp.

Fortunately, she maintained consciousness. She wrenched herself away from him and ran out of the apartment without clothes. She knew that Eric meant to kill her this time.

Blood was dripping all over her face and body by the time Emmaline reached the streets. He intended to kill her! If she hadn't run he would have killed her, over that good-for-nothing slut.

A patrol car was cruising the block just as she ran out of the building. The patrolman stopped the car and a huge, muscular, Black cop jumped out. He took off his coat and wrapped it around Emmaline. Sobbing, she was able to tell them what had happened.

The three of them went back to the apartment, finding Eric back in Emmaline's bed with Ruby. The two cops pulled Eric out of bed and gave him the worst beating of his life. Ruby ran screaming into her room and locked the door behind her. The White cop stood over Eric and said to him, "Motherf——r, you had better get your ass the hell out of Mega City by the time we get back here tonight. If we hear or see you again, you are gonna' be one very dead bastard."

He turned to Emmaline and said gently, "Get your clothes and whatever you want to take with you for now to the hospital. Later if you need to come back for anything, we'll come with you."

It was all she could do to wash some of the blood off and get some clothes on her body. Her head and face were so swollen that they took her straight to the hospital. From there, the policeman took Emmaline to a friend's apartment.

Emmaline was in no condition to return to work and her friend advised her to apply for welfare. Not wanting to be a burden, she dragged her battered and bruised body to the nearest welfare office and was given emergency help.

The next job that Emmaline obtained was in a bar where some of the top Black drug kings socialized and conducted business on a daily basis. Deadly merchandise was left under the bar and would later be picked up by someone else. The man would always give Emmaline a tremendous tip. She lost her job there when the Federal agents raided the bar, found the drugs and closed the bar forever. A grocery store was soon operating from the premises.

While Emmaline was going through her miseries in Mega City, down south in Mississppi her two brothers and mother were going through a few of their own.

Fletcher, her oldest brother, had been drafted into the army four years before. Now, he was being honorably discharged and headed for his mother's house. His brother, Lionel, had stayed at home the entire time. No branch of the armed services wanted him. A smooth talker, Lionel learned how to be a lady-killer of both married and single women. Needing fine clothes to accomplish his low-down deeds, he broke into Fletcher's locked trunk of good clothes.

At first, Cissy protested, but as time wore on, she grew tired of fighting Fletcher's battles and shrugged the situation off. Lionel knew as well as she did what Fletcher was capable of doing to him.

When Fletcher finally arrived home, exchanging cursory greetings with his mother, he immediately headed for his trunk. He lifted the lid with an almost child-like anticipation at the thought of wearing his almost new civvy clothes. The army had helped him keep the fine physique he'd had when he was inducted into the service. It was time to show it off. He wanted to get out of the drab khaki uniform he'd been forced to wear for the past four years.

The horrible shock wave that went through him as he looked down at the dirty, ragged, rumpled garments that lay in the trunk turned him livid with a red-hot anger.

He stormed downstairs to the kitchen to confront his mother. She had the only other key and she must have let Lionel have it, he thought to himself.

"Why the f—k did you give my trunk key to that lazy bastard, Lionel?" He glared at her as though he wanted to kill her.

Fletcher was walking toward Cissy menacingly and his mother remembered the brutal beatings he gave Emmaline with her approval. She knew he was angry enough at this moment to beat her, his own mother, without hesitation. He was fully grown, muscular and at least a foot taller than she.

For once Cissy was really frightened.

"I tried to talk him out of breaking into your trunk, but he wouldn't listen. He said you might die over there and all those good clothes would go to waste." She wasn't going to protect that lazy bum's ass. Lionel had the same menial factory job she'd got him as a kid. He didn't even try to do better. Every cent he could rake and scrape together went to those nasty hussies who let him use them for a few lousy pennies. He didn't contribute anything for his room and board no matter how she had to struggle to make ends meet.

When Fletcher turned away from her and went back to his room, Cissy breathed a sigh of relief.

Cissy would have liked to warn Lionel, but she didn't know where he was at the moment.Too bad she thought. She fixed herself a plate of food and something to drink, carrying her dinner up to Emmaline's old room then locking the door. Fletcher was in his room getting ready to do battle. No telling what he would do, he was very particular about his clothes and had worked very hard to accumulate a nice wardrobe. Carefully packing them away with cedar scents, before he left, he'd given her a key and instructed her not to let anyone near that trunk unless he should happen to die.

Well, Cissy thought, I am now washing my hands of the whole matter. Be it fist or weapon, I don't want Fletcher coming after me.

She propped the pillows up on the bed, sat back, relaxed, and enjoyed her food. After the last mouthful, she fell asleep.

Fletcher was busy looking through his dufflebag for a nine millimeter gun and bullets that he had stolen from the army's ammunition supply. Carefully loading the gun, he stuck it in his belt and went downstairs to wait for Lionel.

Three hours later, Lionel came into the darkened house. He ran straight upstairs to the bathroom, not seeing his brother in the livingroom. Fletcher waited to see where Lionel was headed. He laughed to himself as he heard Lionel farting loudly, in the bathroom. Perfect.

Fletcher hid by the cellar door, waiting for the right moment. He knew Lionel carried a pistol and would not hesitate to use it on him, especially if he had any idea that his own ass was in danger.

Lionel messed around with other men's wives and girlfriends, and was always in trouble. There were two times when he was caught off guard once when he was in bed with someone's wife and once when he was in another man's toilet. Both times he had his pistol nearby and told the men that he would kill them if they did not leave him alone.

Fletcher listened to hear the bathroom door squeak open. The dirty sucker usually left the toilet door open to stink up the whole house, even when the family was eating. No matter how much anybody complained, including his mother, he still did that. Fletcher could kill him for that alone.

Lionel did other nasty things, too, such as drinking milk, soda and juice straight from the refrigerated bottles and containers, leaving a sickening saliva smell around the bottles and maybe something he picked up from dirty women.

As soon as the bathroom door squeaked, Fletcher crept silently to the bathroom door. Lionel was sitting on the toilet seat, nodding off, his pants around his knees. The smell of the defecation had already filled the air, rankling Fletcher's nostrils. He wanted to vomit, but just then Lionel jerked himself awake. The wave of nausea passed quickly and he stopped in front of the open door, gun ready to fire. Before Lionel could reach for his gun, Fletcher fired nine bullets into Lionel's head.

Fletcher took his gun, dufflebag and ran.

Cissy came out of the bedroom only after she saw from the bedroom window that Fletcher had left the house. He might have shot her, too, if he had realized she was still in the house.

The paramedics took Lionel to the hospital where he shocked everybody, including the doctors, by staying alive. His head swelled up as big as a watermelon, which made Cissy ill to look at each time she visited him in the hospital. It took almost a year for Lionel to recuperate. He was determined to live and get even with Fletcher.

****

Emmaline went back to Mississippi, again, in 1974, as a surprise. She went up directly from the airport, to the front door in a cab, knocked on the door. When her mother opened the door, she looked hard at Emmaline, and said, "What are *you* doing here?"

Emmaline, hurt to the core by her mother's words and attitude, turned on her heels without a word, got back into the same cab and went over to her friend's house. Knowing where her daughter was headed, Cissy called there soon after she arrived.

"Bring your ass back here, Emmaline, don't be like that. Come on back home."

Emmaline, believing that her mother had had a sudden change of heart, returned home. Cissy let Emmaline in saying, "I was just surprised you were here".

Wanting desperately to believe her, Emmaline reached out for a hug, but her mother pulled away from her. Emmaline was hurt more than ever, but she stayed anyway and went to her old room. She had bought her mother a new outfit. When she unpacked her bags and gave the new clothes to Cissy, she was very pleased. Emmaline thought that maybe her mother had had a change of heart.

Those thoughts came crashing down to earth with a gigantic thud when Cissy woke her up the next morning at four o'clock, shaking her by the shoulder.

Her mother said brusquely, "I woke you up, because I'm goin' to work now and I'm not leaving you in my house."

Emmaline packed her bags and went to her friend's house, not bothering to tell her mother when she left town.

She did not speak to her mother for two years, and, when she finally did call her to see if she was all right, her mother would cut the conversation short and hung up.

****

1978

Cissy's illness

In 1978, a neighbor called Emmaline and told her that Cissy was very ill with cancer.

As soon as Emmaline got in the door, Cissy said cruelly, "I don't need you down here. I don't want you to do anything for me."

Emmaline stayed anyway, trying to help Cissy by cleaning the house and cooking for her. Her mother followed her around watching Emmaline's every move.

"Why are you following me?" Emmaline asked.

"I'm just watching my belongings."

Grossly insulted by her mother for the millionth time, Emmaline packed her bags and left again.

She went to the same friend's house where she'd gone before.Cissy called there and told Emmaline's friend to tell her not to leave there, because she might never see her mother alive again.

"I feel sorry for the way I treated her," Cissy told the friend.

Emmaline ignored Cissy's request and returned to Mega City, again. It was difficult to keep forgiving such purposeful cruelty.

That December, Cissy's doctor called Emmaline to say that if she didn't return to Mississippi within 24 hours, she would not get another chance to see her mother.

Short of money, a numbers banker (one of Emmaline's friends), gave her a thousand dollars to make the trip.

Cissy was in the hospital, and knew she was dying. She apologized to Emmaline.

"I'm sorry for all the bad things I said and did to you, and for what Fletcher and Lionel did to you. Please forgive me."

Emmaline told her mother she always forgave her, which is why she kept coming back home.

As Lionel stood by Cissy's hospital bed, she spoke to him in a soft weak voice.

"You should have given Fletcher's clothes to me to wash and iron, while they were still in good condition. You didn't have to wear them until they were all tore up and filthy, then put them back in the trunk like that. I don't blame him, I would feel like killing you, too. You better get down on your knees and thank God that He saw fit to let you live. I want you to promise me that you will forgive your brother and make up with him."

Lionel wanted to hit his mother, but he was still afraid that Fletcher would come back and finish him off. Right now, he was just waiting for this bitch to die. He wanted to get her money before Fletcher found out she was sick and came back home.

"Forget about Fletcher, ma. He don't care nothing about you. He should be here now," Lionel's voice was mean and bitter.

"I ain't gonna' die until I see Fletcher. Where is he? When is he gonna' get here?" Cissy had lost so much weight that she looked like a skeleton. The cancer was eating her insides out.

Lionel had started practicing his mother's handwriting since she became ill, and was writing out checks against Cissy's account. He cashed the checks at the gas station, even though the signatures did not match her card there. The proprietor attributed that to Cissy's illness.

The bank wasn't as forgiving, the checks bounced. Lionel promised to pay the money back when his mother died. The manager agreed as he certainly couldn't get his money back if Lionel was in jail.

Cissy died within hours of Emmaline's arrival. Fletcher had found out somehow and showed up at the hospital minutes before his mothers death.

Emmaline took her mother's illness and death very hard. When she left Mega City she weighed 130 pounds. In a matter of a couple of weeks, Emmaline was down to 75 pounds. Cissy's death nearly killed her as she could not accept it.

The doctor gave her sedatives and said that if she didn't get herself together, she would be buried right beside Cissy.

Lionel was only glad to see Emmaline because her signature was needed on the insurance policy, which provided five thousand dollars for each of the three of them if they paid funeral expenses. If Fletcher had not shown up, Lionel and Emmaline would have split the fiftteen thousand dollars, since only one other signature besides Emmaline's was needed.

Lionel and Fletcher rushed the undertaker into having an immediate funeral for Cissy, who had stipulated that only fifteen hundred dollars be spent for her funeral. She did not want the undertaker to get all of her money, she wanted her children to have it.

But Fletcher and Lionel claimed that fifteen hundred dollars was too cheap. Instead of contributing five hundred dollars each, they would each contribute fifteen hundred dollars.

He and Lionel decided to spend more money for a better coffin and masses of flowers for the church. The two brothers then tricked Emmaline into paying the full amount by herself, having her front the funds with no intention of paying her back.

Even before Cissy was buried, Fletcher and Lionel started fighting over everything, the house, Cissy's fur coats, jewelry, pots, pans, dishes, etc. Emmaline was so upset that she stayed over at a friend's house, crying and carrying on.

Two days later, she went back to her mother's house to pick out what she wanted to keep. Everything was gone. Her two half brothers had stripped the house of most of the good pieces selling them for what they could get. What Lionel couldn't sell, he gave to his girlfriends.

Emmaline hurried to the hospital to get her mother's belongings, a gold wedding band, a necklace and a few dollars in her purse. Cissy's hands were smaller then Emmaline's, so Emmaline put the rings on the necklace and wore the necklace around her neck.

She went back to the house to sleep, but her careful efforts to keep her brothers away from her failed.

Locking the door and securing a chair under the door knob was just not enough to keep Fletcher's tremendously big feet from kicking the door open. He strode defiantly into the bedroom, gun in hand, looking very much like the devil himself.

Standing over her, he pointed the gun at her head.

"Bitch, gimme' those rings you got hanging around your neck. Hurry up, or I'll blow your motherf——g brains out, like I did Lionel. The only reason I ain't gonna do it is, he'd like that. More money for him.I got the check for the house today. He don't know it, and it's gonna help pay me back for all those clothes he messed up. You don't deserve any money, whore".

He snatched the necklace off Emmaline's neck, then hurried out of the room, getting out before Lionel came back in the house.

As soon as he left, Emmaline jumped out of bed, packed her bags and headed to Mega City this time to stay. She did not want to go back to Mississippi until she was in her coffin.

****

1983

Agatha's train lover

Agatha sat on the train, commuting to Scarsdale, feeling bored.Looking at her reflection in the window of the moving train, she could see the man beside her. He was gazing steadily at her, and she felt flattered and giddy. She pretended not to notice him, but when she turned her face back, he spoke to her.

"Beautiful day, isn't it?" The man was still gazing at her.

Her voice was a little nervous as she answered, fingering her handbag with useless little gestures.

"Yes, it is." Agatha made direct eye contact with him for the first time that day.

"My name is Gregory." He stated this, sure of himself. On previous trips, he had noticed her staring at him, in spite of the wedding band she wore. It made no difference to him, he wore a wedding band also. He had a beautiful wife and a beautiful baby girl.

"Oh, my name is Agatha." She was now looking at him hungrily.

Gregory almost started to back away, when Agatha blurted, "Would you like to have sex with me? I saw you staring at me before."

Although women had approached him before, he didn't often accept their offers. This woman seemed almost desperate for a man.

"I beg your pardon?" He looked at her questioningly.

"I said, would you like to have sex with me?"

Gregory smiled broadly at Agatha. What the hell! He supposed it wouldn't hurt to accommodate her. She looked harmless enough. Probably led a sheltered life and now had an impotent husband.

"I might want you to do things you won't want to do." Still smiling, he put his hand under her skirt. She put her newspaper over his lap and felt his crotch.

"Follow me," he said, pleased. They left their newspapers on the seats and he took her into the toilet. Agatha stood inside the tiny booth with her mouth open.

"Come on in, women come in here all the time," he lied as he locked the door. Gregory taught her a few tricks that day that even she hadn't tried before. He was even kinkier than she was.

For two weeks, Gregory took full advantage of Agatha's willingness to please him. He took her into empty train cars or in the toilet to do whatever his perverted heart desired. The look in her eyes told him that he had the upper hand and could call all the shots.

Emmaline was Agatha's captive audience, as she raved on and on about Gregory. Agatha would have been horrified to know that Emmaline felt sorry for her. Agatha thought that Gregory was going to divorce his wife and marry her.It was hard to believe a woman of her intellect would put herself in such a mortifying situation.

Even while Agatha bragged about Gregory to Emmaline, he was dialing the phone to call her.

Moreaver answered the telephone and buzzed Agatha.

"Who is it?" Agatha questioned with annoyance in her voice. She didn't want to be interrupted while talking or thinking about Gregory.

"It's Mr.Gregory Otere." Moreaver answered.

"Oh, thank you."Agatha's voice was now syrupy sweet.

Picking up the phone, Agatha gestured for Emmaline to leave the office.

"Hello, Gregory. What a pleasant surprise. I was just talking about you," Agatha said coyly.

"Really? What were you saying? Something bad or something good?" Gregory was fishing for a compliment.

"You know I wouldn't say anything bad about you," she said, smiling broadly. "I think that I am pregnant, can you deal with that?" Agatha was sure Gregory would marry her.

Emmaline stuck her head in the door for a minute to signal to Agatha that she was going out to lunch. Agatha winked at her and waved her out.

Meanwhile, Gregory's hair was standing on end.

"Look Agatha, I'm very married and I love my wife. I don't want to hurt anybody."

Agatha, in shock, hung up on him, trembling. He called her right back.

"What's wrong?" Gregory sounded puzzled.

"I just can't take this. I'll talk to you another time." she hung up again.

When Emmaline came back from lunch, Agatha told her what happened.

Emmaline said, "You did the same thing to me."

Agatha apologized to her, over and over again. Then proceeded to unload her problems on Emmaline. She kept Emmaline in her office until ten minutes to five, talking about Gregory. Saying that she thought she was pregnant by him.

She knew that if she were pregnant, it couldn't possibly be her husband's baby. He was busy with some young chick at his office. By the time he got home at night, he was impotent and couldn't do anything. Try as she may, none of her tricks could arouse him.

Not that she loved or even wanted him, but he had a prestigious job in a well-known corporation, which paid for the beautiful house they lived in with three children.

When Agatha was pregnant with her firstborn daughter, she tried to commit suicide by taking an overdose of barbituates. Her husband was brutally abusing her and forcing her to do perverted sexual acts, facetiously calling them 'acts of unconditional love'. He called an ambulance, which saved her life by pumping out her stomach in time. The doctors noted the bruises on Agatha and called the police. The police put Agatha's husband, Daniel, through a series of questionings that ended only when Agatha refused to press charges.

After that, Daniel behaved himself. Agatha told him that if he started abusing her again, she would go to the police herself and press charges. The baby survived, miraculously, and they had two more children. Daniel lost interest in Agatha after the birth of the third child and began having extramarital affairs with co-workers half his age.

Agatha went to college at night, earning a MBA, then passed the civil service exam for "caseworker" and was hired. Her first supervisor was Ida Rifkin who became her first woman lover.

****

1985

BCS' new Deputy Director

In 1985, two years after Sheba left, BCS still had no Deputy Director. All the backstabbing and terrible lies that Violet Gray inflicted on Sheba gained her *nothing*. The powers that be realized that Violet knew very little about the new system. Sean and Steve Beck decided to get someone from the outside. So when a friend of a former commissioner called to recommend a friend of his, the man was hired.

Agatha resented not being able to choose her own assistant, but Sean had tried for the past two years to get Sheba back. Sheba had the experience needed for the job and the expertise for the new system. She had been in testing for three years. If Agatha had not been sexually involved with so many individuals in top management, she would have been dumped long ago.

The newly hired Deputy Director was Arthur O'Neill, an extremely handsome White man. He always wore a suit with shirt and tie, and looked good sitting behind the desk. Arthur O'Neill did not know *anything* about the job he accepted. He needed a job badly after pounding the pavement for the past year or so. He bluffed his way into the job, knowing a little about personal computers, because his son had one at home.

He would go to meetings and sit there trying to understand what was going on. Agatha wouldn't answer any of his questions, she told him to ask somebody else. Violet Gray resented him and made it clear she wanted nothing to do with him. He began to feel very unwanted.

Until Ilene Levinson came into his office.

As Ilene swished down the hall to the new Deputy Director's office, Victor Garelick watched her and thought how ridiculous she looked. Why Agatha continued to let her get away with dressing like that in the office was a matter to be reckoned with. Nobody else could get away with ignoring Agatha's 'dress code'.

Ilene's skin was very pale and pasty, right on down to her legs, which she liked to keep uncovered. In her mind, this was very sexy. Her hair was almost waist-long, and dyed a brilliant, yellow-orange color that showed dark roots. Today she had on a bright yellow and black skin-tight outfit. The entire staff wondered how she managed to get into her clothes. Ilene stayed on a diet of black coffee and cigarettes, sometimes getting down some yogurt or cottage cheese. She kept herself extremely thin for her 'moonlighting' job. Ilene had on a waist cincher that pushed her breasts up so high, Victor thought that she could suck them herself.

He stared at her until she turned the corner and went into Arthur O'Neill's office. Victor then went into his own office and closed the door. Minutes later, he was asleep laying on top of his desk, snoring.

Arthur O'Neill looked up from his desk at Ilene as she swished her rear end into his office.

Ilene plopped down in the chair in front of his desk. First she stood for a few moments posing for him, to let him feast his eyes on her wonderful body. All of her clothes had that 'bedroom look' including her blue jeans. They came straight from Felix's of Hollywood.

In case one didn't notice, Ilene bragged incessantly about how gorgeous she looked and the way she had power over every man she met.

To her face, some of the staff would agree with her, but behind her back, they tore her apart. Even now, as she sat before the deputy director, crossing her legs sensually and gazing longingly into his eyes, she was the subject matter of discussion in Nellie St. James' office. The boned waist cincher and the knee-length girdle that were underneath her tight low-cut top and skin tight pants were a hot topic.

"Something I can do for you?" ONeill asked as politely as he could without breaking out in uncontrolled laughter. He looked at the ludicrous pants and blouse, and thought he could feel his hair standing on end. This woman was flirting with him. There was no way he would risk any kind of intimacy with *her*. She looked like a veteran prostitute, a candidate for any and all sexually transmitted diseases.

Ilene, still gazing into his eyes, thought that he was as thrilled about her presence as she was with his. She mistook his annoyance for desire.

"Mr. O'Neill," she purred, "I want to welcome you to BCS. If there is anything, anything at all I can do for you, just let me know."

"Such as?" he asked with raised eyebrows.

"Oh, you name it. Anything at all," she purred. Arthur thought he might offer her a dish of milk to lap up.

"You must have something in mind." He wanted her out of his office. Ilene gave him a queasy feeling. She couldn't keep still, crossing and uncrossing her legs, trying to bring his focus in on her crotch. Each time her high spiked heel, also from Hollywood, hit the floor, it made a irritating, squeaky sound that made his teeth grind.

"Well, one hand washes the other around here. I can do a lot for you and vice versa. I work hard and I like to be rewarded, and I can reward you in return. Agatha knows that and will tell you so." Ilene was using all the tricks she knew that worked on most other men, trying to be as irresistable as possible. She was making him very nervous because she obviously wanted to force him to make a pass at her, but he didn't. His face was expressionless as he stared at her.

"Your name?" he asked quietly.

"Ilene Levinson", So, she thought, he *is* impressed.

"Miss Levinson," he said in very low tones, "I hope you don't mean what I think you mean."

"What do you think I mean?" Ilene spoke a little louder, but kept her voice controlled. She wanted special favors from him and in return, she was ready, willing and able to give *him* 'special favors', particularly the 'house specialty', as she called her best trick. Arthur was an exceptionally goodlooking man and deserved the best she could offer him. Even if he wanted to close his office door and take care of business right now, it was fine with her.

He looked at her coolly. She wasn't going to trap him into saying something stupid, besides, he was already tired of her games. No way he wanted this worn-out bitch.

"Right now, I'm thinking I have a lot of very important work to do. I can imagine you do too, since you have explained to me how hard you work. I'll tell Agatha about your generous offer."

Ilene stared at him, stunned. He was turning her down! Not knowing what to say or do, she slowly got on her feet and almost stumbled to the door.

She always carried her disposable douches with her and a dozen or so condoms. At night she worked the singles bars after leaving BCS. Her fees were from fifty dollars up, depending on what the client wanted. Male or female, her place, their place or a motel. That's why she was always prepared. Besides she had very definite plans about moving up at BCS and she never knew when Steve Beck might send for her. Top management was always horny and "politicking" was the only way up. Only a fool and a mule worked hard.

Agatha, in a way, was one of Ilene's mentors. Both Ilene and Agatha practiced bisexual sex, as did most of the top management's men and women. Agatha had informed her that she went to 'political' parties, where as many as four or more people were in bed together, exchanging partners. She had promised Ilene that she would get them to invite her.

After Ilene and Agatha had become intimate, Ilene began to Lord it over the other staff members there, including Agatha. She was one of the clique that called Sheba"Miss Goody Two shoes", a prude, "Miss Sanctimonious" and other choice names, because

Sheba did not share in their love of pornography, obscene humor and orgies. They laughed at Sheba because she was a loner and wanted nothing to do with them. It was funny to them, also, because Sheba thought she was going to get ahead through hard work, the very same work that had created promotions for her supervisors at BCS.

While Ethel was there, Agatha knew that Sheba knew more about the adminstration's procedures and policies than anyone else there, including herself. Sheba had trained staff on operations long before Agatha worked for the city. Agatha liked Sheba and she liked her work. She also respected Sheba, who didn't gossip about other staff. Agatha was hoping to score with "Miss Goody Two Shoes". Sheba really excited her. Many times she had tried to let her know what she wanted, but either it went over Sheba's head or she ignored what Agatha was saying.

Ilene suspected how Agatha felt and hated Sheba more. When Sheba left BCS, Ilene knew she would be next in line to take over. But Arthur O'Neill burst that bubble of becoming Deputy Director.

Besides games with Agatha and other top management, Ilene's best friend at work and the world at-large was Louisa, a Black woman who worked at BCS. It took Ilene many months to convince Louisa to go to bed with her. Shortly after that, Louisa broke up with her husband. He left, taking his son with him, when someone told him about his wife's affair with Ilene. Louisa did not know that the, 'someone' was Ilene. Feeling quilty, Ilene gave Louisa money to help makeup for her husband's salary.

Ilene went through the office halls, saying loudly, "I just love Louisa, I just love Louisa."

Louisa sat at her desk, working, ignoring Ilene, totally oblivious to what she was saying. She seemed not to let anyone or anything bother her. Being a soft-spoken, dignified young woman, she never raised her voice to anybody. Her appearance was average, almost plain, and completely free of makeup, an exact opposite to Ilene. Few staff members knew she was an alcoholic who kept a bottle of liqueur in her desk drawer at all times. Ilene was trying to introduce her to cocaine, but Louisa refused. Two bad habits were two too many.

Ilene was doing good business selling the cocaine to Agatha who in turn, sold it to top management. The so called Yuppies couldn't function without it. That's why, when receiving unexpected phone calls they sounded utterly 'spaced out' they really *were* 'spaced out'

Agatha allowed Ilene to break many departmental policies and get away without any reprimand. Ilene completely stopped doing anything that resembled work once she got Sheba's job. She forced her subordinates to write all of her reports and memos, while she sat at her desk, doing her inch-long fingernails in bright orange polish. Ilene had a binder full of pornographic magazines which also kept her occupied when she wasn't talking to Lousia about sex.

Ilene knew her subordinates deeply resented her for many reasons. They didn't like what she had done to Sheba, and they didn't like what she was doing to them. They missed Sheba sorely, but they were helpless to do anything about it. Agatha had given staff strict orders not to contact Sheba under any circumstances or she would demote them and send them back to the centers.

All except Odessa, who was Agatha's protege from the Women's Forward Movement. Agatha was the chairwoman of the board of this committee and took advantage of the power it gave her. It helped her to get the director's job away from Ethel Green. The group was mostly Black women as the *most* discriminated against and, in Agatha's mind, rightly so. They didn't have the brains to start an organization like this. She founded this group, a White woman, but she used and abused the power it gave her.

Agatha loved the way the Black women in the group looked up to her. It made her feel like a goddess, over slaves. She told Emmaline that she used the Black women to fuel her power to reach the position she had reached in the City government. Agatha's power base expanded, built on the frustrations of the women's inability to receive promotions because of the color of their skin.

Somehow she manipulated certain people to give her and the women that were 'true followers' higher positions, and keep all the others, in a hopeless struggle, trying to carve out their own niches in the management empire. Agatha made glorious promises of what she could do for them, but in reality, she capitalized on the economic misery that brought them into the organization in the beginning. When any Black woman seemed to be making progress within the organization, ready to take over Agatha's position, she quickly used the old rationale, "Divide and Conquer".

She would set the other women against her, thereby maintaining the power and tightened her own grip.

Agatha applied the same theory to BCS. Divide and Conquer. She had gossiped to the staff about Ethel, and tried to turn every one against her. If the staff said anything negative about Ethel to Agatha, Agatha would repeat this to Ethel. Emphasizing that all of the staff hated her. They did *not* hate Ethel, they may not have loved her unconditionally, but they really did not hate her.

But it finally worked. Steve promoted Ethel to get her out of BCS, and she was glad to leave.

Once in position as director, Agatha proceeded to unleash her sadistic approach to management on BCS. She outlawed all sick leave without a doctor's note, yet allowed Ilene to stay out anytime without a note. Ilene's time sheets were given directly to Agatha. Not even Agatha's secretary, Moreaver, saw those forms. There was no way legally that Ilene could have as many sick or annual days as Agatha approved.

The picture became clearer to some staff when there was an important meeting out in a local site that Ilene had to attend. One of Ilene's subordinates called in to ask a question. Agatha called out to the site to speak to Ilene about it, but Ilene was not there and had not been seen that day, so Agatha called Ilene's home. The phone rang twenty times when finally a man groggily answered it. Agatha asked to speak to Ilene.

Ilene's voice was overwrought with anger when she came on the phone. "What the f—k do you want? Why are you always calling me at home?"

Infuriated by Ilene's tone, Agatha shouted, "You were supposed to be at an important meeting today. Instead, you are home in bed f——g some man!"

"You've got some f——g nerve calling me at home. What I do at home is none of your business. I called in sick this morning. Don't you ever call my house again, for any reason!" She banged the phone down as hard as she could in Agatha's ear. The man in bed with her was one of her steady customers and needed to be with her that day. Besides he was paying triple her usual fee.

When Agatha put the phone back in its cradle, she looked cheap. She sat there fuming for a few minutes, then called Violet Gray to go to the site and substitute for Ilene. The incident was then forgotten.

After that, Ilene simply got worse, she walked all over Agatha. She worked her "johns" more than she worked at BCS. Her reports, signed by her, were being written entirely by her subordinates. Ilene had no idea what was going on until she scheduled team meetings and was updated by her workers.

Ilene was confident that Agatha would not do anything to her as she knew too much, just as Agatha's superiors would not cross Agatha because *she* knew too much about them. Agatha did anything she wanted to do, but she stayed on, much to her staff's chagrin. She was an expert in humiliating *everybody*.Agatha bragged to Ilene that if she were demoted, she would tell the newspapers enough to make the front page of the *Daily Mega News.* She vowed to drag the whole agency down with her.

Top management knew of Agatha's inconsistencies of character. They also knew she was very disturbed emotionally and very unstable. They used this, sometimes, for their own lurid objectives. It was a deliberate choice on management's part to leave Agatha, an extremly dangerous personality, in that position of power. With so many jobs at stake, including their own. this was a proven fact of managment's unsound judgement and inability to think beyound their libidos.

Behind management's back, Agatha called them a "bunch of dumb bastards" and bragged that she would have Clovis' job one day. She claimed she was much smarter than Clovis, and that a Black woman did not need a job as important as the one Clovis had.

Although Clovis called herself Black, she had skin whiter than Agatha's. Clovis capitalized on the fact that she had Black blood in order to help advance herself under the affirmative action program, which provided equal opportunities for minorities and women. She did not believe in EEO for other Black women, she promoted only young White males, some of whom were reportedly her lovers.

Clovis supported Agatha when she gave Ilene Sheba's job. Steve and Sean's interest in Sheba had annoyed Clovis. Both men respected Sheba, and spoke highly of her whenever they got the chance. Even though she left a few years ago, they still remembered her. Clovis was sick of Sheba. She was very dark, not all that pretty and her clothes were nothing special. What the hell did these White men see in her? Especially Sean. He was tall, intelligent and very good-looking. Sean could have almost any woman he wanted, except Sheba. Clovis was very upset about that, she felt that Sean was her own personal property.

After all, she was the person responsible for getting him every promotion he had received since he came to work for the city. Sheba didn't want Sean, moreover, she didn't need Sean. Sheba had Bob all to herself, he was a one-woman man. Clovis had a husband, too, just as Sean had a wife. So what? She still loved Sean, and always would. Sheba could go to hell.

Instead, Clovis heard that Bob and Sheba, along with Sheba's daughter and grandchildren, had gone to live on a fantastic ranch somewhere in Texas.

Sean was the reason Clovis helped Ilene get Sheba's job. He was also the reason she helped Ethel stop Sheba from getting other promotions.Although both Sean and Steve wanted Sheba, Sheba seemed to be completely unaware of what was happening around her. There are a number of conspirators in the plot to sabotage Sheba and all were ecstatic when she left her job at BCS several years ago. Sean had been devastated.

When Sean heard about Sheba leaving, he was beyond furious. He had to quiet himself down to a quiet rage. The day he called Agatha into his office to confront her, he thought he would kill her.

Sean got Agatha on the phone.

"Come to my office," he said, his voice taut with anger.

"It's twelve o'clock and I'm on my way out to lunch." Agatha spoke nervously. She knew what Sean wanted.

"I don't care what time it is, you get in here *now*!" His voice sounded more and more like thunder.

"I'll be right there," Agatha replied meekly. Clovis would have her ass if she was insubordinate to Sean.

Walking into the room, Agatha could feel his fury all around the office. His livid eyes stayed on her from the moment she entered the room and sat down. She was going to wait for him to order her to be seated, but her knees began to buckle and she welcomed the chance to sit.

Agatha was fortunate, she only felt Sean's anger. But Sean's feelings went a lot deeper than just plain anger. Inside, he was seething and hurt. The Sheba he knew was a very decent woman, working hard and constantly to do the very best she could do on every project assigned her, completing them before deadline dates. She never asked him for anything. The recent reports that she handed in were very good, even though Agatha had complained about them. Sheba's reports weren't any worse than anybodys else's, including Violet Gray, the head supervising field monitor.

Just before he ordered Agatha to his office, he snorted some coke, calming his nerves down. He could imagine his strong hands around Agatha's scrawny neck. Sean wanted very badly to hurt her.

He managed to hold himself back as she walked into his office. She was visibly nervous and looked as though she was about to burst into tears. That bitch, Sean thought as she eased her rotten ass into the chair. She was nothing but bad news. He had heard she had sex with anybody and everybody in management who would have anything to do with her, even flirting with him once. There were steady complaints from her own staff and other sections, including the more than ten grievances at this point. He had spoken to Clovis about her and wanted to get rid of her, but Agatha had some connections somewhere high up in city government.

Now this. Sheba had quit her job because of Agatha. He thought highly of Sheba, despite Clovis finding out and taking him to task about her, simply because she didn't like the way he looked at Sheba.

Sean didn't even know Sheba had left until he went through that morning's mail. He came upon a letter from Sheba. At first, he felt a warm strong emotion rushing through him.

It was as though she was in the room with him. No one else made him feel this way. As he read the letter, he became more flushed, but because he was getting angry. Angry at that sick bitch Agatha.

She was notorious for abusing staff emotionally, with unjust negative criticism, insults and a bitchy rejection process, such as "get the f—k out of my office" or "I don't give a flying f—k what you want." Her reign of terrorist tactics made her many enemies, but she seemed not to care. Agatha bragged about the amount of power she had. She said she could do anything and get away with it, no one dared to stop her.

Sean kept Agatha in his office for four hours.

For all of those four hours, every question, statement and answer was about Sheba. In the end, he ordered Agatha to apologize to Sheba and get her back to BCS.

When Agatha returned to her office, she told her secretary she was going home.

"You look upset," Emmaline said.

"Damn right, I'm upset. All he talked about for four hours was Sheba, Sheba, Sheba. I am sick and tired of hearing about Sheba."

"What did he say?"

253

"He wants me to get her back here." Agatha reflected on that last statement. She really wanted to get Sheba back there herself, more than she cared to admit to anybody. When Sheba had said she was leaving, Agatha's hair stood up on end. She didn't believe Sheba would go through with it, sure that Sheba was bluffing.

Three hundred times, that's how often Sean called Sheba's name to Agatha. Maybe even more.

Agatha slammed her desk drawer shut after removing her bag and went home. She did not want to hear Sheba's name again.

But that wasn't the end of it. Nearly every day, Sean prodded Agatha to apologize and ask Sheba to come back to work. Again and again he checked Sheba's work against the other supervisors' work, their work was no better than Sheba's. In fact Sheba's reports were far better than the rest. He brought this to Agatha's attention over and over until she finally admitted her mistake, saying that the other supervisors had college degrees. Sheba only had two years in college. Sean said that it was more important to have workers who knew what they were doing than to have an unknowledgeable staff member with a degree.

Agatha got Emmaline to call Sheba and tell her to call Agatha. Sheba refused, she told Emmaline to tell Agatha to put it in writing. She had already been a victim of Agatha's devious tactics. If Sheba called Agatha, she would brag to everyone that Sheba was begging for her job. Agatha wasn't about to put anything in writing, she was too afraid of being sued.

When Sean realized Agatha was not going to apologize to Sheba or make any attempts to get her back, he made up his mind to get rid of Agatha. He began to formulate a plan for her demotion and eventual transfer. Then he would contact Sheba himself and ask her to return to BCS.

But Clovis did not want Sheba back and when Sean discussed his plans with her, she refused to go against Agatha. Clovis wanted Sean more than she wanted any man on this earth and Sheba was the only one who could possibly keep Sean from her.

"Let's face it, Sean," Clovis glared at him, then snarled, "You want to screw Sheba."

Sean flushed, but looked at Clovis coolly for a minute, then said in a strained voice, "It goes a lot deeper than that."

"Is that why you stopped seeing me? Are you making love to her?"

"No. I'm not. I only want her, I'm not sure she wants me, but I can't make love to anyone else right now, not even my wife. I'm sure she loves her husband very much and she won't cheat on him."

"Even if Sheba came back, I'll make sure she never gets anywhere in ths department, and I won't approve a transfer out for either of you." Clovis reached for her tissues and blew her nose loudly.

Sean felt sorry for her. He didn't hate her, he knew she loved him and always tried to give him whatever he wanted until now.

"Don't take this out on her. She hasn't made any passes at me, ever. I wish she had," Sean said with a heavy sadness in his voice.

"I don't care. The fact that you want her and you don't want me is enough. I can do a lot for you. She can't do anything for you, except hold you back."

Clovis had spittle in her mouth and it disgusted Sean, he turned away from her.

He headed for the door, saying, "Let's talk about this when you calm down."

"You stay here, I didn't dismiss you yet." Her voice was mean and low.

Sean opened the door.

"If you want to talk business, I'll stay. If you want to get personal and nasty, I'm leaving. I don't need this, I have enough problems."

Clovis leaped up from the chair. "Please stay, don't go. You know how much I love you. If you stay and forget about Sheba, I'll promote you to the next level under me, just do what I want you to do and you'll go right to the top with me. Please?"

Sean stopped in his tracks. Hell, he thought, why not? He closed the door and stayed.

****

<u>1989</u>

The BCS Predators

Emmaline sat at her desk in BCS, eating her lunch. She didn't eat too much these days. The litigation she had going against Agatha was wearing her down. She was suing Agatha for all the indignities she had made her suffer, including sexual harrassment and abuse. Emmaline wanted Sheba's help as her lawyer had said she needed at least one witness. Nobody else was willing to help. The staff hated Emmaline and Agatha equally. They weren't about to risk losing their jobs for Emmaline.

Emmaline had tried to contact Sheba by mail, but received no answer. Sheba never gave her a new telephone number after finding out it was Emmaline harrassing her by telephone.

Sipping her coffee slowly, she didn't notice that the taste was not quite right. When she had come back from the deli with her lunch, she left it on her desk while washing her hands. Nobody was around to see Agatha slip some white powder in Emmaline's coffee.

Three hours later, Emmaline was dead. The paramedics carried her body to the nearest hospital and pronounced her dead there.

****

Hortense Mussels sat at her huge oak desk, seething, a letter from Sheba Dunn clutched in her large, red, scaly hand.

The nerve of that bitch!

For the past two weeks, Sheba and Hortense had been corresponding by mail. Sheba was in Texas with her husband and family and wanted a copy of some sort of workbook. She claimed it contained the formulas for various projects that she had created, developed and implemented all by herself.

Originally, the request for this workbook had been directed to Gertrude Hardwick at BCS, to whom Sheba had loaned the book. Mrs Hardwick never did return the workbook and had used the material contained in it. Mrs.Hardwick then took full credit for the creation and development of Sheba's work, even receiving a promotion as a result. Somehow Sheba had learned that even Agatha was refusing to let the woman part with the material.

Sheba then wrote to the Commissioner and informed him of the situation in the letter.She explained her reasons for leaving the way she did and the horrible situations that Agatha put her through.

The Commissioner was appalled but instead of using his own judgement, he decided to call a meeting of top managers to resolve the situation. Most of them, male and female, were at one time or another Agatha's sex companions.

Sean and Ethel were staunch in their opinions that Sheba was an excellent worker. Both of them had given her outstanding performance evaluations every year that she worked for them. Agatha maintained that Sheba was a lousey worker, still trying to justify her actions.

"Is it true, Agatha, that Mrs. Dunn requested training several times and you refused to comply? Also, is it true that you or Mrs. Gray never answered questions about the work? As supervisor, it is an important part of your job to train subordinates. You don't tell them to get the hell out of your office and go ask someone else. When you feel that someone isn't functioning well in the job, it is mandated that you have conferences with that individual and if disciplinary action is necessary, you take it up the chain of command. You don't just call them into your office on a whim and demote them. There are several other things in this letter that we will be going into at a later date. In the meantime, Miss Mussels will try to placate Mrs. Dunn."

Hortense Mussels read Sheba's personnel file and saw that Sheba was American born and from the south which meant of course that she was Black. Immediately, she decided Sheba was probably a stupid woman and that she would treat Sheba accordingly.

Hortense, although she was Black, did not think of herself as being in the same ethnic group as American Black people. She fiercely believed that her White blood and her West Indian background made her superior to American-born Black people. Every chance she got, she would enlighten anyone who would listen. Once in a while, she would trap an already biased, gullible, non-Black person into agreeing with her.

Of course, she in turn, was told off quite a lot. The reality was that Ms. Mussels, had a very low opinion of herself. When her captive audience did not agree with her, she would just talk louder and longer.

When the Commissioner brought her in on Sheba's dilemma, it was her big opportunity to prove something to him. Hortense wanted to display her strength and power. In order to do that, she would have to humiliate Mrs. Sheba Dunn, while resolving the problem Sheba had created.

The letter she worded to Sheba was pointedly geared to make Sheba shut up and leave the Commissioner and everyone else alone.

Dear Mrs. Sheba Dunn,

We have searched for the book that you claimed belonged to you. There is no trace of it anywhere in BCS.

I suggest you put that book behind you and enjoy your retirement down there in Texas with your husband and family.

Sincerely,
Hortense Mussels

When Sheba received the curt and unfriendly missive from Hortense, she knew exactly what she was trying to do, devastate her into a submissive silence. Well, Sheba thought, I'll just shake you up a little bit.

Dear Ms. Mussels,

I don't understand the reason for your letter, especially since I have already written the Commissioner rescinding my request for the book.

As for your facetious directive that I enjoy my retirement, who do you imagine you are? I will live, if I choose to do so, working or not working.

My life will always be enjoyable and nothing you say or do will make it better or worse.

Sincerely,
Sheba Dunn

When Hortense received Sheba's letter, she was shocked. She hadn't believed Sheba would answer. She was supposed to be too cowed to answer Hortense's letter.

After about three weeks, Hortense decided to answer Sheba's letter. She did not want Sheba to think she had the upper hand. The reply was worded almost exactly like the first letter she had written Sheba. Spitefully (wallowing in her own ignorance of the situation),she signed off with the same closing lines to show Sheba that nothing she had written mattered to her.

Hortense had seen Sheba on occasion, in the past, and was intensely jealous of her. There was no way anyone would guess how old she *really* was. Sheba Dunn was attractive and looked at least 25 years younger than her age.

On the other hand, Hortense was frequently mistaken for an older woman. Hortense's looks left much to be desired, with extremely protruding teeth that even braces couldn't help, kids used to call her 'horseface.' The front teeth protruded even when her mouth was supposed to be closed. The two upper front teeth had an unusally large gap between them wide enough for an adult finger to easily slide through. Hortense's eyes were nervous and her eyeballs darted around constantly, uncontrollably, especially when she was upset about something, which happened frequently.

Her figure was slim and had a smooth line when she wore a girdle, but her hips and backside were right at her waistline, which was very close to her bust. Hortense had long legs, shaped like spaghetti, wore her skirts and dresses with the hemline just reaching her knees. She felt that her legs were one of her best assets and dressed to call attention to them.

Ms. Mussels was 5'10", and walked with a stiff legged gait that originated from her hips, without bending her knees. This made her steps short and nervous. The roots of her hair were dark, the rest of it was dyed "Brilliant blond". She had frequent outbursts and no matter how obvious an error she made, Hortense never admitted she was in the wrong. Her ticket to the job she held was one of her politically powerful relatives.

As Mildred Cantor stated, "BCS had an army of dirty, lowdown, dumb bitches and Hortense was one of it's leaders."

****

<u>1991</u>

The fatal day

The Commissioner, David Martinson, sat at his desk, head in hands, guilt washing over him like giant ocean waves. He knew that what had happened to Sheba was unfair, to say the least. His job, head of such a large agency, put him in the position of making a lot of bad decisions. There were just too many corrupt individuals to deal with, and they all had top drawer connections with which to pressure him. These sleazy staff members didn't mind cutting throats to get their own way, so he always caved in to the pressures.

Even his own *mother* called him a wimp on occasion, but he got even with her for that mistake. The first chance he got he placed her in a nursing home and he never went to visit her.

As a man, he was a nondescript wimp. His coloring was insipid and watery. Were it not for the position of power he held, it was doubtful if *any* woman would have tolerated him. All through school and college, he worked very hard to get high grades. He made many sacrifices to get his PhD. Many times he considered giving up, but the idea of having power over some of the people who made his life miserable drove him to reach his goals.

He joined political organizations to make friends with all the 'right' people. Now, after all that, his conscience was whipping him for the first time in his life.

Here was a decent woman, trying to make an honest career for herself, and the greedy and devious actions of some very selfish people had made her a victim.

Oh well, he sighed to himself, that's all a part of life. He put Sheba out of his mind, at that moment, forever.

****

It was midnight. Seven of them sat around Steve Beck's conference table, looking so grim and fierce that anyone who happened to walk in the office unexpectedly would have trembled at the sight. They were discussing Agatha.

Hortense spoke up, breaking the deadly silence. Her protruding front teeth loomed larger than life as her mouth opened. The reflection from the florescent bulbs above the table made them gleam like mini-spotlights.

"What are we going to do about her?" She asked.

The Commissioner blinked. He was the weakest link in the chain. Hortense was glaring at him.

"What can we do?" He asked in a wavering voice. "She told Ilene Levinson that she poisoned Emmaline Spenser. When she contacted Emmaline's daughter, she made her sign all sorts of papers. One of them refused the hospital the right to an autopsy. The body was sent directly to Mississippi for burial. Agatha got the daughter the twenty-five thousand dollars for a death in the office. There was no argument from the daughter after that. Ilene told Steve. That's why we're here now."

"Why don't we report her to the police?" Sean inquired.

Steve spoke up, "I called her into my office this morning. She told me if we turned her in she would involve all of us. If she is demoted or transferred from her position as director, she will tell everything to the newspapers."

"It's her word against ours." Clovis said defensively.

Steve Beck looked up from the pen and paper he was toying with, and glared at Clovis like she was a fool.

"First, the media will believe any down side that *any*one says about city employees. Second, Agatha claims she has pictures, tapes, written notes, memos, etc."

"Shit! Do you believe that? That's impossible." Clovis countered.

The Commissioner interjected.

"Remember, we were all very high at those parties. Agatha drinks a lot, but she could have been faking. I personally think she has *something*. What do you think Steve?"

Steve cleared his throat.

"I think she should show us something. If she can't, then we can decide what action to take."

Silent up to now Ethel spoke in a monotone.

"She has something. The last time I was with her, I saw a small tape recorder in her bag. I asked her about it. She said it was for meetings only."

"Yeah! The group meetings we have after work." Steve enjoined angrily.

"You mean she can ruin all of us?" The shock on Ethel's face chilled the other six people at the table.

Silence reigned again while the conclave considered their options.

Hortense, her face hard and cold, said in a terrifyingly emotionless voice, "We have to kill her. There's no other way to deal with her. She admits to being a cold-blooded killer herself."

At the mention of the word kill, horror showed on *all* of the other faces.

Hortense continued.

"For some time now, Agatha has been behaving quite irrationally. Besides that mess with Sheba Dunn, the rest of her staff is constantly complaining about her verbal abuse and total lack of control. There are at least fourteen grievances filed against her. Labor Relations is constantly on the phone complaining that she never shows up for conferences. They say that when they call her to find out why, she screams and hurls vile obscenities at them. In light of that and what we know she's capable of, I don't think we can afford to ignore her any longer, hoping the situation will somehow resolve itself. Agatha must go."

"And how do you propose we go about the dirty deed?" Steve questioned.

"Shoot her, stab her, poison her, run her over with a diesel truck! What the hell difference does it make?

Just as long as we get rid of the c—ks——g bitch!"
Hortense said with venom.

"Are you volunteering to do the job?" the
Commissioner sneered. "After all, it was your idea."

"I think we should pull straws." Hortense was
deadly serious.

No one was laughing. The subject was being given
serious thought. Although they didn't mind sabotaging
other people's careers for no good reason, they were
willing to consider murder to save their own jobs.

"All right". Steve was still very grim. "Let's take a
vote. We are all intelligent adults, we must give
considerable thought to the consequences no matter
what course we choose to take. Bear in mind that this
is a last-chance situation, one way or another. If
Agatha lives, she will eventually ruin us all. If we
continue to let her abuse staff, that situation, too, will
blow up in our faces. On the other hand, if we demote
or transfer her, she claims she will go to the media and
that will, of course be a huge disaster. We wouldn't
even be able to get a job in McDonald's as waiters
after that. First we will take a vote on what action we
will take. What ever we decide must not be discussed
with anyone outside of this room. If we vote to kill her,
then we will have to draw straws to select the person to
do the job. That person will do the job, or resign. That
includes the Commissioner and myself. The only other
alternative to all this is mass resignation by the seven
of us."

Sean absorbed the entire meeting and decided to
speak up.

"I think you are forgetting something."

Surprised, Steve looked at Sean. "What did I forget?"

"Suppose you select someone who would rather quit than kill? Then that person might take Agatha's side and there would be two people to worry about." Sean looked steadily at Steve. He didn't like him at all. Steve had had something to do with Sheba's leaving BCS.

"True!" Steve answered. "Do you have a solution for us?"

"If we do kill Agatha, then that person would also be able to ruin us," Sean replied.

"Are you suggesting that we forget about her and her threat? Are you prepared to start your career all over again from the bottom?" Hortense demanded an answer.

"If Agatha goes to the media, we could be ruined. That's a possibility. At least we would not go to prison, but there's a pretty good chance *she* would, for extortion, as well as murder. If we kill Agatha and we are caught, we will *surely* go to prison, for premeditated murder in the first degree." Sean said firmly. "I for one am against going to prison. I'd rather be free and start over."

The Commissioner stood up.

"Sean is right. No matter how careful we are, something might go wrong. What we've been doing is certainly scandalous, but not illegal between consenting adults. As long as the police do not find drugs on our person or anywhere in our possession, there is no crime. For the moment, we will let Agatha remain where she is until we can come up with a more suitable solution."

Everyone, except Hortense, looked relieved. She turned purple with rage.

"You can't let her get away with this. She is a no good slut and she will get us all into trouble."

"Only if she is demoted or transferred," Sean reminded her. "She wants to remain where she is, in BCS as director."

The Commissioner nodded and said, "We'll give everything that we discussed here tonight some very serious thought. I'll let you know when we will meet again. Should something happen in the interim, I'll call an emergency meeting.Remember, nothing said here is to be discussed with anyone out side of this room."

The meeting was over.

****

Just as Rafael was thinking that Agatha was the weirdest, wildest, most spaced-out woman he'd ever met on Planet Earth, she got up off the leather couch in her office and started putting on her clothing, She was completely nude and stopped in front of the full-length mirror there to examine herself.

"What are you doing?" Rafael called to her.

"Getting dressed." She had her underwear on now and was about to step into her skirt.

Rafael was on the couch, nude, They both had been snorting coke and drinking alcohol. Ever since Sheba had left, he'd begun using every kind of drug except heroin and he was beginning to look emaciated.

He had transferred to County Bureau #105 because Sheba was there.When Sheba transferred to BCS, *he* transferred to BCS. Now he was looking for another job because he was getting fed up with Agatha. He used her for sex and the drugs she bought for him.One of these days, he was going to give her a good beating because of the way she had treated Sheba. A few times, when he lost his temper, he had smacked her around, nothing *much* and she'd acted like she enjoyed getting hit.

Rafael looked at Agatha's flabby gray skin and wondered why he had started up with her. Agatha had him convinced there was nothing wrong with snorting coke, he was already a hard drinker. Never having used cocaine before, he was delighted that he could get high without as much alcohol. When he got used to coke, he started mixing it with alcohol as did Agatha.

The more she drank, the wilder she got, the wilder she got, the better Rafael liked her.Right now, she hadn't snorted enough coke or drank enough alcohol to get her really wild enough to satisfy him. His appetite for sex was tremendous or maybe it was all in his mind. Either way, he did not want to leave just yet.

"To hell with you." Rafael was pulling at her clothing. Agatha screamed at him. "It's getting late. My staff will be coming in soon." Agatha continued putting on her clothes.

"They don't come in until eight o'clock, it's only seven now. Besides, they took all your staff away except for your secretary and that whore Ilene."

Rafael was getting angry now, so he got up off the couch and went over to her. He grabbed her roughly and tried to pull her clothes off again.

"Stop it, Rafael!" She yelled at him.

"Motherf——r. I say you are going to do what I want you to do, right now." Rafael was shouting now too.

Agatha was furious also so she slapped his face as hard as she could. Who did he think he was ordering around?

The slap made Rafael go berserk he wasn't used to women hurting him physically. He beat her with his fists, maniacally. As she succumbed to the heavy, constant blows of his huge fists, he did not realize that she had stopped moving. In fact, she had stopped breathing.

By the time he realized what he had done, Agatha's bulging eyes were glaring coldly up at him. Her mouth was frozen in a scream. Blood was all over both of them.

Rafael became fear-stricken and sat back on the couch, trying to figure out what to do next.

He stumbled to the locker in the corner of the office and took out two towels. Everything was wiped clean, as clean as he could get it, including Agatha. Putting on his clothes, he didn't notice that both his wallet and keys fell out of his pockets, his hands were shaking that badly.

Finally, managing to dress himself, he took one last glance at Agatha and ran out of the office.

Rafael ran down the four flights of stairs, managing to dodge the cleaning men, and raced the five blocks to the subway. Reaching the turn-stile, he discovered he had no money. It dawned on him at that moment that his wallet was still with Agatha.

Someone could have already found Agatha, along with his wallet and keys. He leapt over the

271

turnstile.The transit policeman standing nearby went after him, Rafael ran down the full length of the platform, turned and saw the policeman gaining on him. His confused drug-fogged brain made him panic and leap to the tracks.

Just then, a train came rumbling towards him. He stood frozen to the spot, seeing in his mind the train's headlights as Agatha's bulging eyes. The policeman called to him, but was helpless to do anyhing for Rafael.

The newspapers' account first carried Agatha's murder and said they were looking for Rafael as a suspect.

Three weeks later, when police had checked Rafael's fingerprints, the newspapers carried the story of his tragic death, connecting the two cases. Both cases were closed.

****

Even though Rafael had left County Bureau #105 a while ago most of the women were upset for months afterward about the way he died. Some of the people speculated that Rafael committed suicide after he murdered Agatha.

In the lounge, the gossip group at County Bureau #105 put forth their own theories on the subject.

"That bitch Agatha, I always knew she was no good, ever since they caught her screwing that young boy on her conference table." Rachel stated flatly, still eating her favorite meal, collard greens and potato salad.

"You don't know nuthin'." This last remark came from Marie, she was bigger than Rachel and a lot tougher.

Marie continued, "Why don't you just stop bullshitting, Rachel? You are always trying to make people think you know *everything*. Every time you open your mouth, you put your big foot in it, always getting the story ass-backwards. You ain't nuthin' but a nosey bitch trying to bring everybody down to your level."

Rachel stopped chewing and glared at Marie. She wasn't going to take that from nobody.

"Why the hell don't *you* shut up? You're just mad because Rafael can't screw you anymore." Rachel's mouth was full and the food was flying in every direction. The other women looked at her in disgust.

Marie jumped up from her chair and headed for Rachel. Knowing she was in imminent danger, Rachel moved quickly away from the table, leaving her beloved *collard greens and potato salad* behind.

Some of Marie's friends stopped her and took her outside the lunch room.

"Look Marie, if you start fighting with Rachel in there, you might lose your job. You have to think of your three children. So be cool. Everybody knows she ain't nuthin' but a big mouth. Hell, she screwed Rafael herself."

Marie started crying at that, and they took her into the ladies' room.

Meanwhile, downstairs in the back room, Baker was playing cards with some of the men. While Rafael was alive he couldn't get back at him, so he decided now was his chance.

"That lying bastard Rafael got what he deserved. I found out he never screwed Shirley," announced Baker, maliciously.

"Who are you trying to kid? I was with him one day when Shirley invited him over to her house for some real loving!" Marvin growled, chewing on his cigar.

Baker felt embarrassed and remained quiet for the rest of the game. When he came out of the back room, he lit up a cigarette. One thing for sure, Baker thought to himself, he transferred his big ass out of here, following Sheba, even though she was married, but the bastard never got next to her. He smiled to himself. Good for Sheba.

****

1992

Culmination of business

Steve Beck sat behind his monstrous mahogany desk, soaking up the thrill of being in top management and at the peak of maximum, absolute power. This feeling made up for all the times in his life that he was made to feel inadequate because of his lack of good looks. He had even lost his aggravating stutter.

Along with this power, came all the sex he had ever dreamt of having.

Beautiful women who would otherwise not even *look* at him now begged him for favors. All except Sheba. He'd given her every opportunity to come to him, but she never had. She could have had anything she wanted, if she had come to him. It would have been called sexual harrassment, if he approached her, and his job would have gone right down the sewer. Her husband, Bob Dunn, got lucky when he went to work at County Bureau #105. Nobody else wanted to go to work at that local center.

About the time he was feeling his full burst of glory, the phone rang. It was Lou Woods, from the procurement section on Fourteenth street.

"Listen, Steve, did you hear about Ilene?"

"What about Ilene?" Steve asked, examining his just-manicured nails closely. "And you'd better tell me what's up before I get very angry."

"Okay! Okay! Ilene Levinson is in the hospital with AIDS!" Lou said anxiously.

Steve's blood turned to water. He couldn't speak, even the gasp stuck in his throat. His head began to spin crazily. Incredibly, he was beginning to think he was immortal. Taking risks, knowing the price he might have to pay for indulging in casual sex.

Kenny's illness had had him frightened before, but tests a week after Kenny's death showed Steve was negative at the time. Instead of calming down, he continued to play games, like a sexual Russian roulette.

Steve thought that with Agatha out of the way, life would be smooth sailing forever. Now his world seemed to be turning upside down.

"Steve! Are you there?" Lou asked, fright building in him like a tornado getting ready to blow. He didn't know why he should be so afraid. Ilene was Steve's flunky and Steve was known to use Ilene's services on a regular basis. But, unknown to Steve, Lou had used Ilene's services occasionally, just as many other men *and* women had.

"Yes, I'm still here." Steve's voice was suddenly very tired. He was fighting panic every step of the way. All he could think of was running to the doctor for tests, tests and more tests.

"Well, I just thought I'd let you know. Talk to you later." Lou hurried off the phone. He knew Steve was sweating bullets, just like every other man who'd let

Ilene service him. Death was a high price to pay for a few moments of instant gratification.

As Steve sat behind the powerful desk he loved, the life seemed to be draining out of him. He took a mental body count of all the men and women whose sexual amores he'd enjoyed. The number was astronomically high. If he was infected, then all those suckers could be infected too. He never *forced* anyone to do anything. His primary regret was that his wife, and on an outside chance, his kids, might also be infected. They were the innocent parties involved. All the others, including himself, took calculated risks.

For the first time in his life, he had no sure answers and he had no idea as to how to handle the situation. So, when in doubt, keep quiet; when accused, deny everything.

The next day, Steve took a day off and went to see a doctor, without telling his wife or anybody else. He took all the necessary tests for HIV.

A few weeks later, he heard the bad news. He didn't tell his wife right away. It was hard explaining to her that he didn't know from whom he contracted the deadly virus. Kenny might have given it to him or one of the hundreds of other men or women he was intimate with. He just didn't know. All he knew was that *his* moment of reckoning had come. His physician advised him to tell anybody he was or had been intimate with so that they could be tested and if positive, treated. Also the doctor told him to avoid contaminating anyone else.

At first Steve was angry. He was too young to die. His virus had already spread though his body, even though he did not feel ill. According to the tests, he must have been contaminated for at least five years. He could have contaminated Ilene.

Unfortunately, Steve was intimate with everybody he promoted or hired directly, over five hundred individuals. He had absolute power, and as it goes, was absolutely corrupt. His mother had told him many times, "Don't let power go to your head. It can kill you, one way or another. No matter how high you go, you can fall. The higher you are, the harder you fall."

He'd laughed at his mother many times, in fact, as recently as the day before he found out that Kenny was dying of AIDS.

There were a lot of people he had to call. Among them, Ethel Green, Clovis, Hortense, the Commissioner, Sean and many others.

Some of them would be certain to have the virus, such as Ethel. The three of them, Ethel, Kenny and himself, were in bed together several times. There were plenty of other trios like that, Ilene sometimes participated. Now, it weighed heavily on him. He'd gone too far. He had spouted hedonism to all his disciples and they avidly believed him because they were greedy and didn't care what they did to make it to the top.

Steve had to wonder, was there really such a thing as Karma? Was there really a Supreme Being, GOD? If so, was He really watching everybody and paying people back for their sins against other people? Sheba Dunn believed all of this and more. The last he heard of her, she and her family had moved to Texas, and lived on a elegant ranch. Now, Agatha was dead, Ilene was sick with AIDS, BCS was obsolete, everybody in

BCS was demoted or back working in the local centers or fired.

Steve was genuinely glad for Sheba, and sorry that the power he had been given had corrupted him so badly that it seemed to totally dissipate his conscience. He had treated people in an inhumane manner, disregarding any moral standards, codes, or laws because he felt he was above all of that. Well, he had now found out differently, the hard way.

Steve picked up the phone and made his first call about his illness to Ethel Green.

The End

About the Author

Currently, she is the writer of novels, screenplays, and plays. Formerly SAG actress and singer, she had roles in over forty films, TV, off-Broadway plays, etc. She was employed by a large civil service agency for many years.